worship BAND PLAY-ALONG

GUITAR EDITION *Volume 3*

How Great Is Our God

Recorded and produced by Jim Reith at BeatHouse Music, Milwaukee, WI

Lead Vocals by Tonia Emrich and Jim Reith
Background Vocals by Jim Reith and Janna Wolf
Guitars by Joe Gorman
Bass by Chris Kringel
Keyboard by Kurt Cowling
Drums by Del Bennett

ISBN 978-1-4234-1723-1

HAL•LEONARD®
CORPORATION

7777 W. BLUEMOUND RD. P.O. BOX 13819 MILWAUKEE, WI 53213

Visit Hal Leonard Online at
www.halleonard.com

How Great Is Our God

Above All

Words and Music by Paul Baloche and Lenny LeBlanc

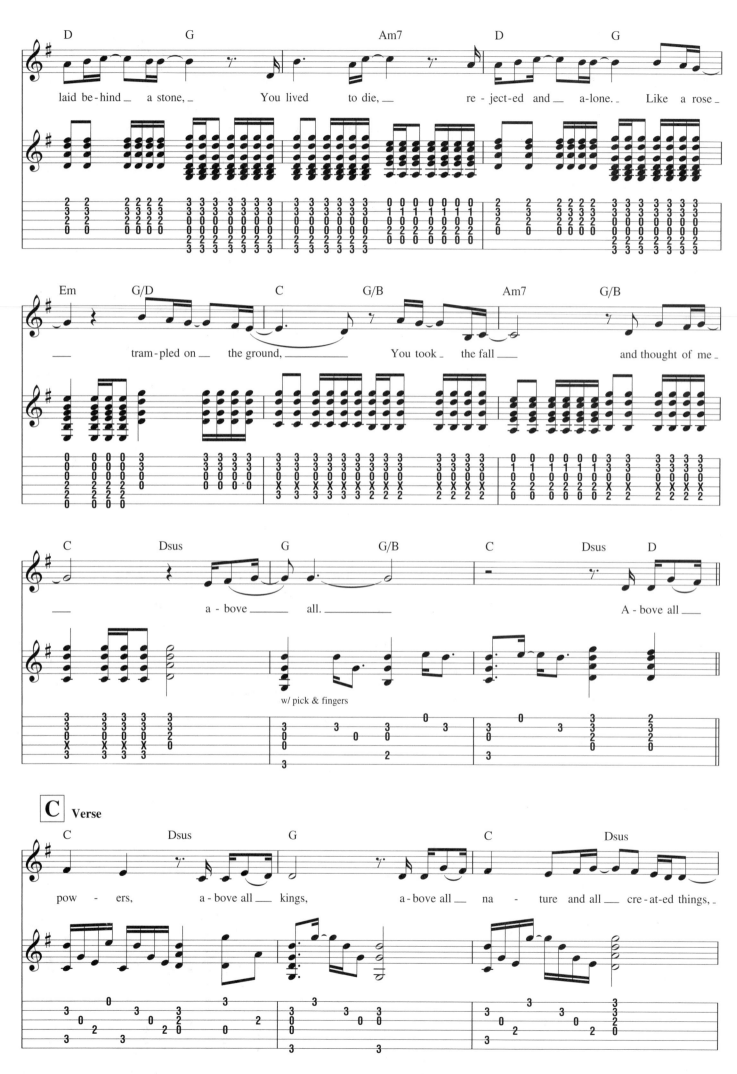

Beautiful Savior
(All My Days)

Words and Music by Stuart Townend

Capo II

In a slow 2 ($\downarrow$ = ca. 52)
Intro

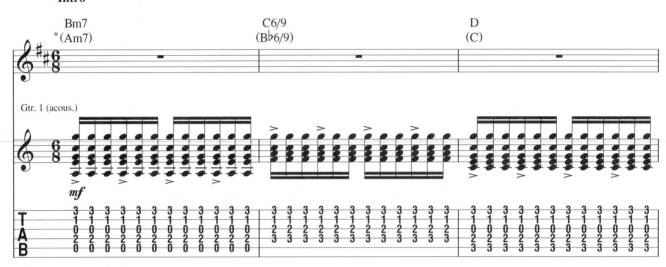

*Symbols in parentheses represent chord names respective to capoed guitar.
Symbols above reflect actual sounding chords. Capoed fret is "0" in tab.
Chord symbols represent overall harmony.

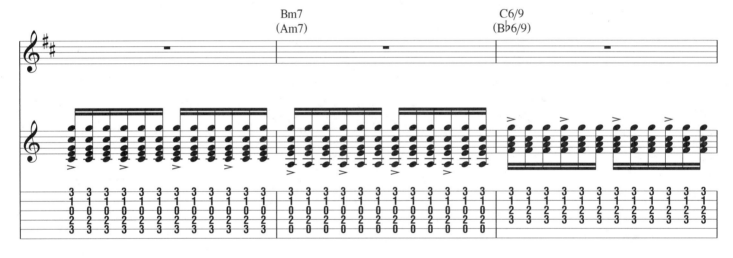

A **Verse 1**

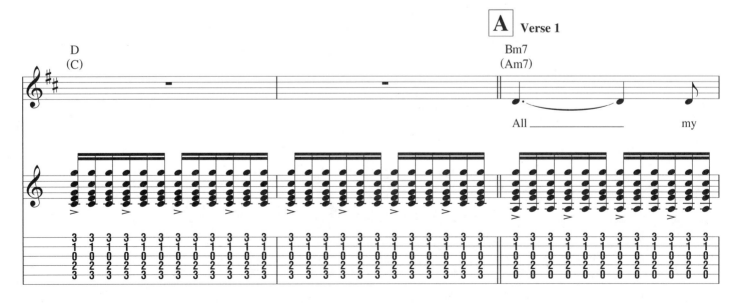

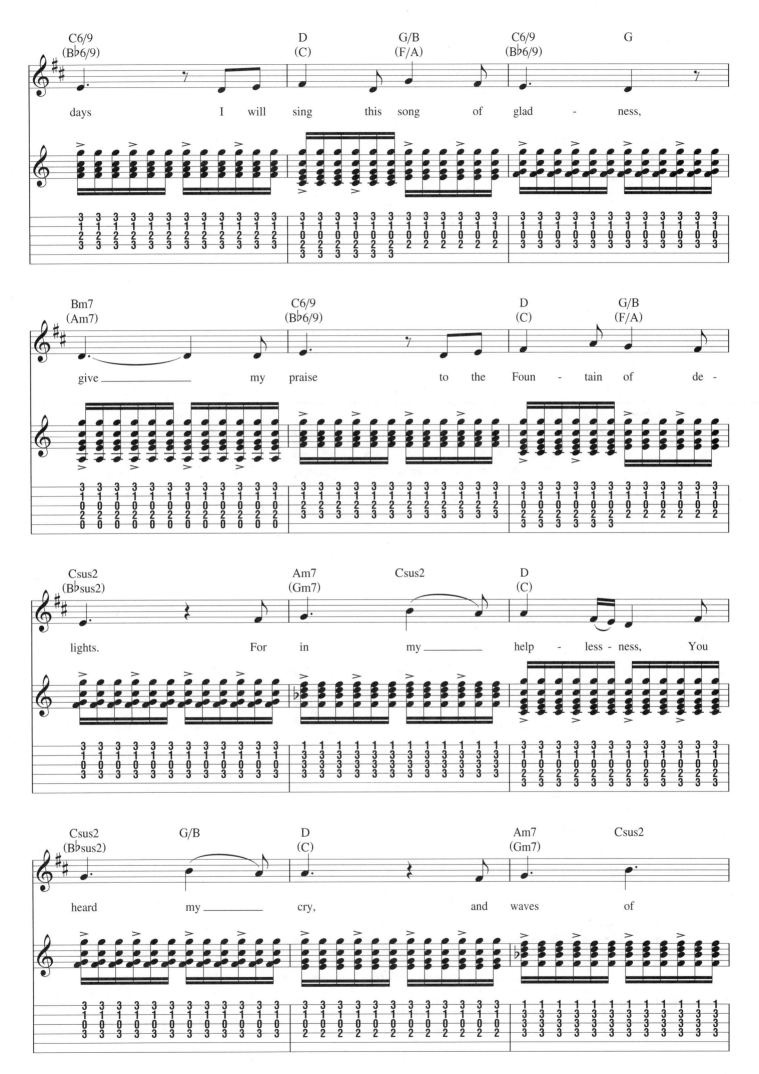

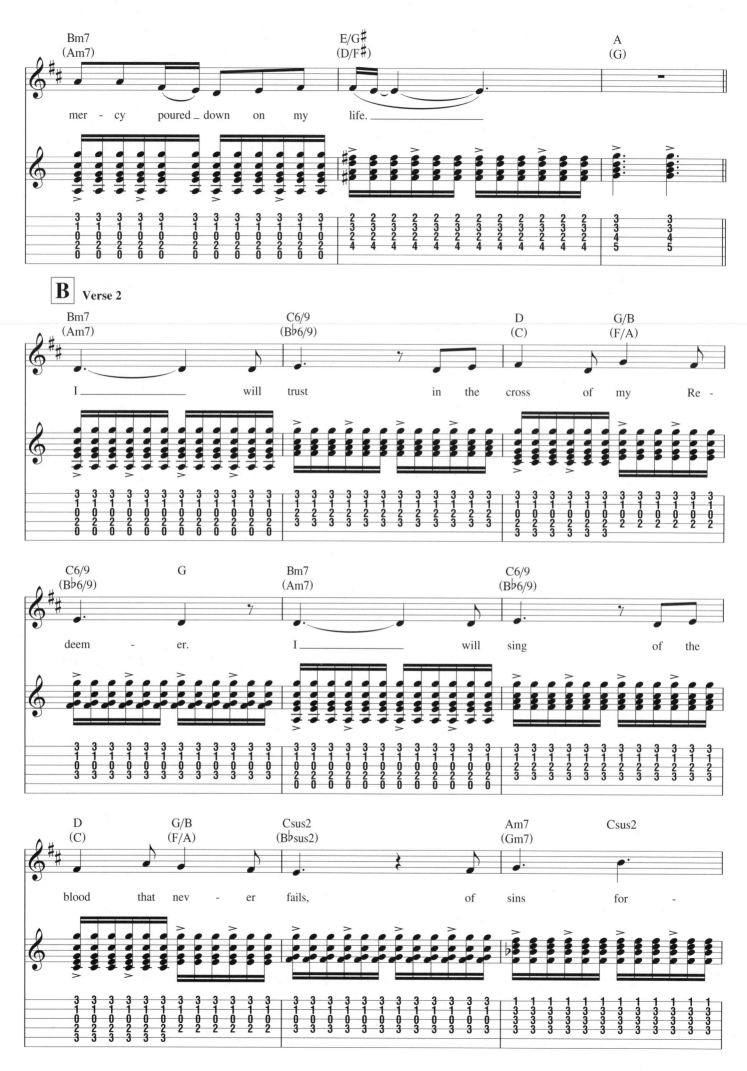

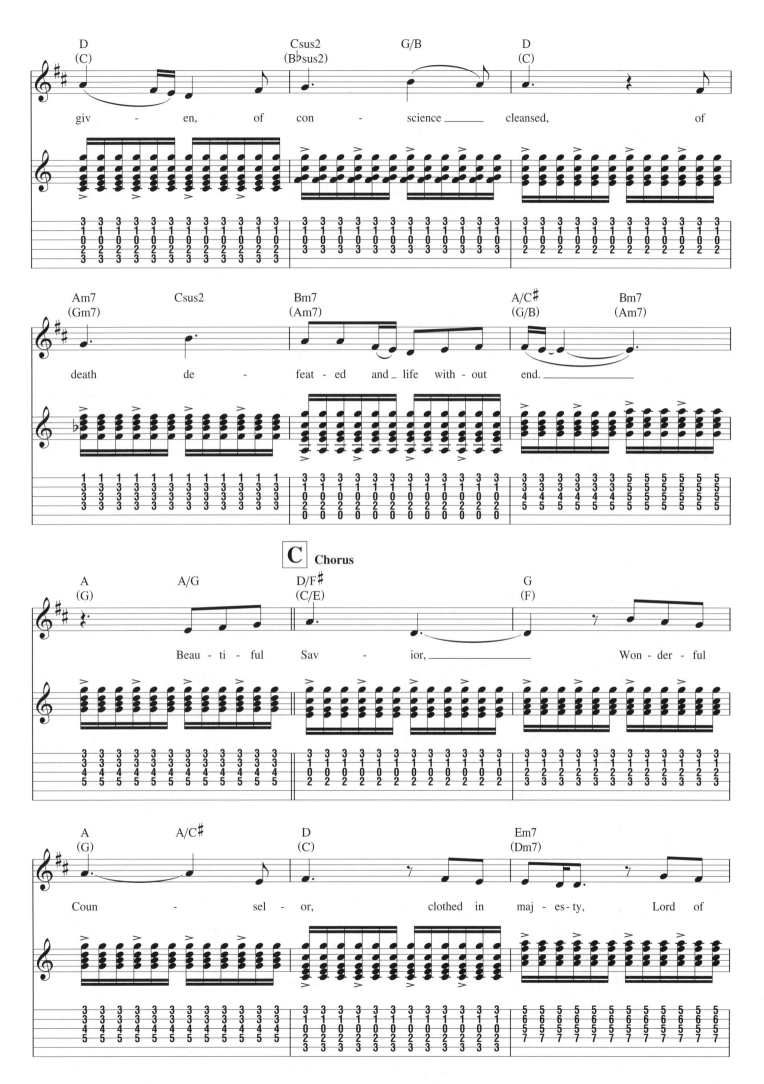

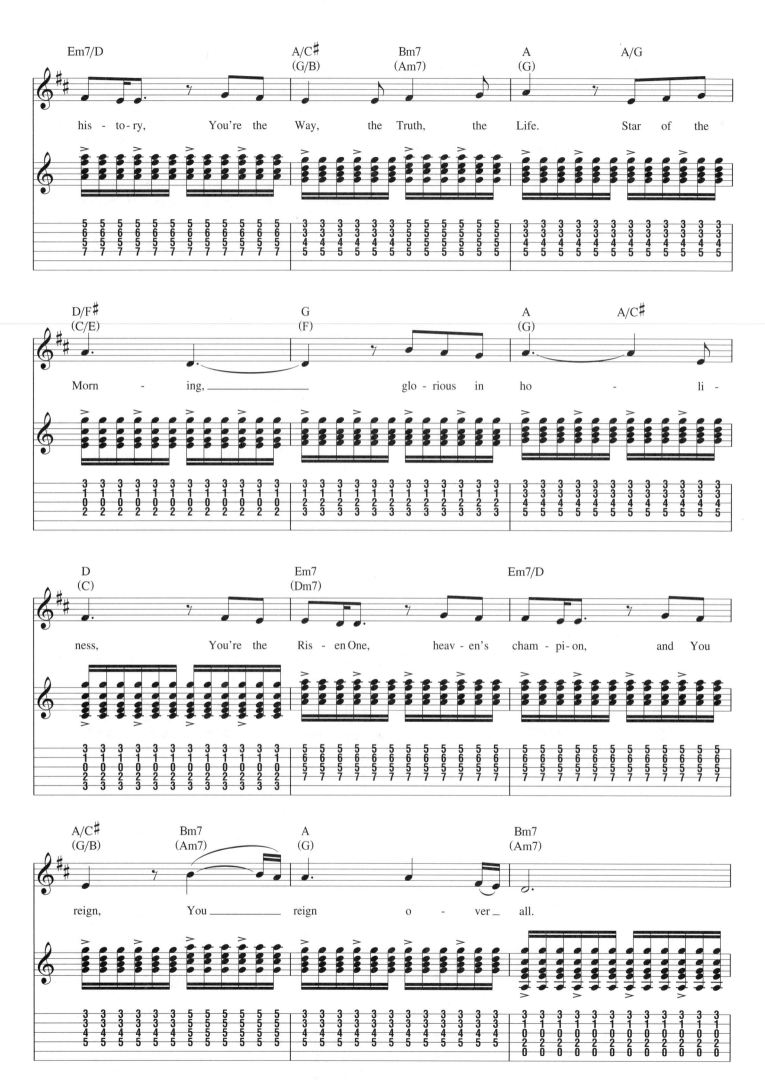

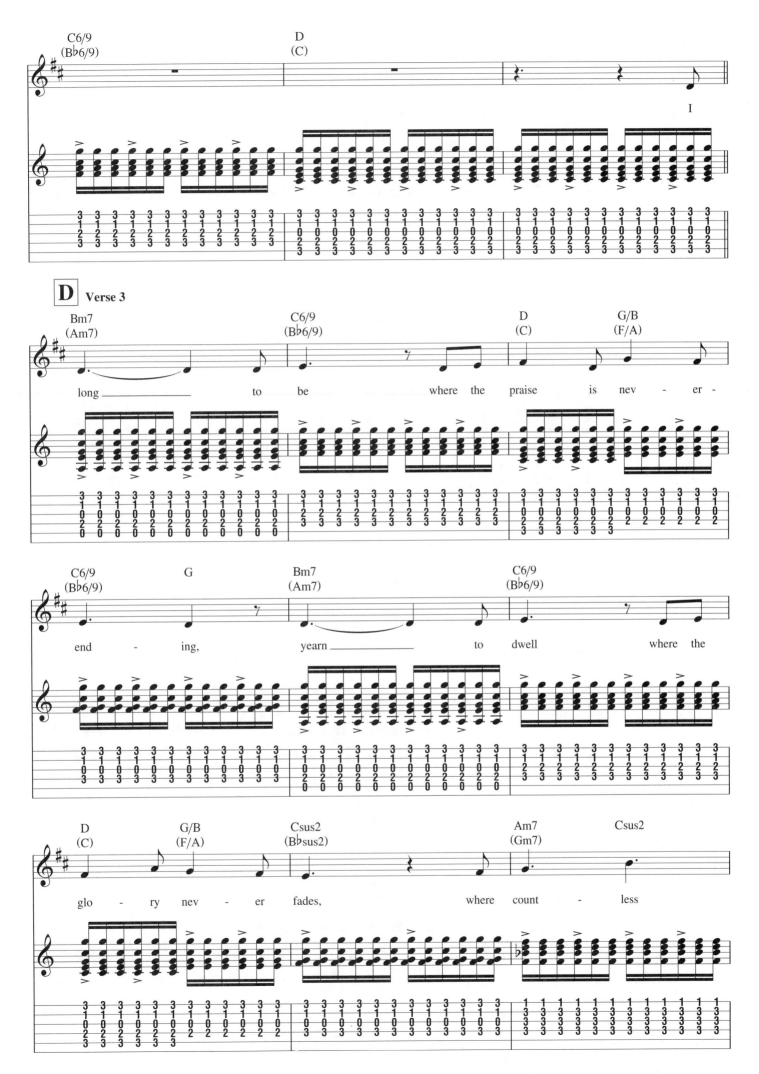

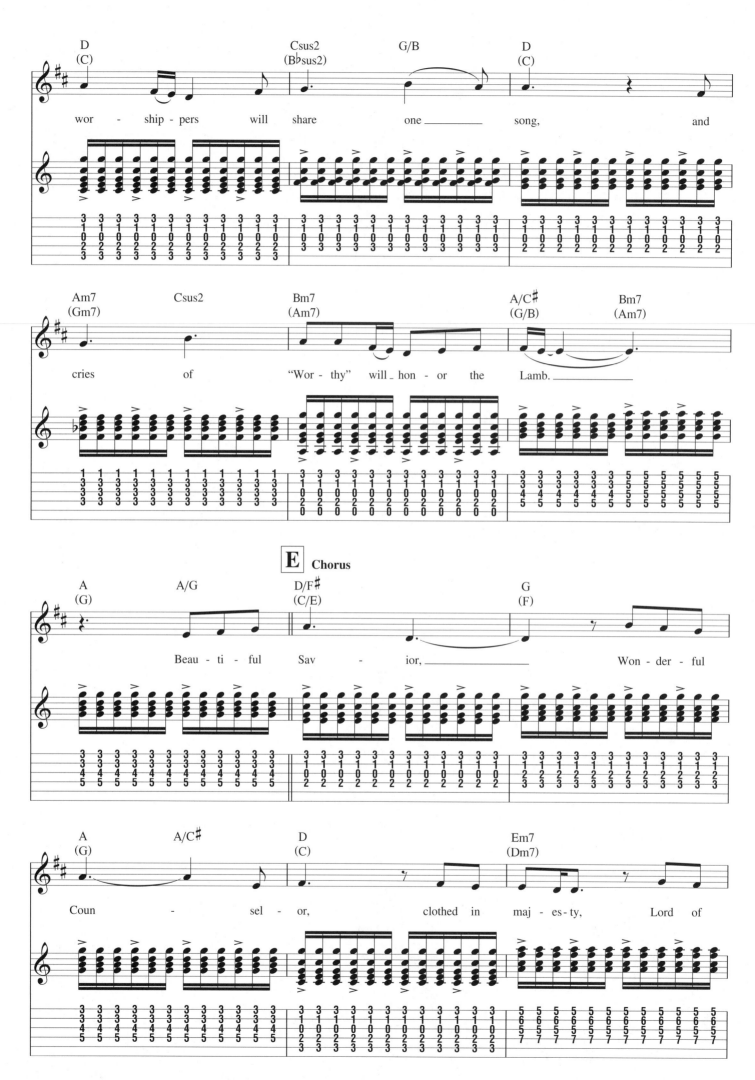

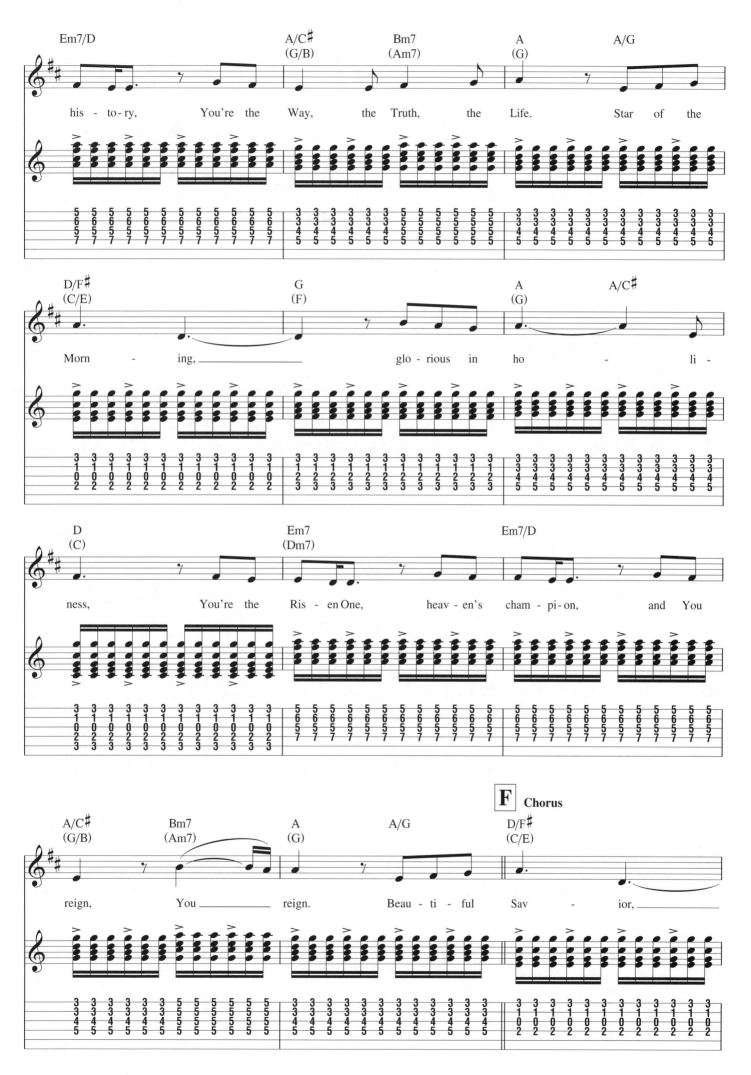

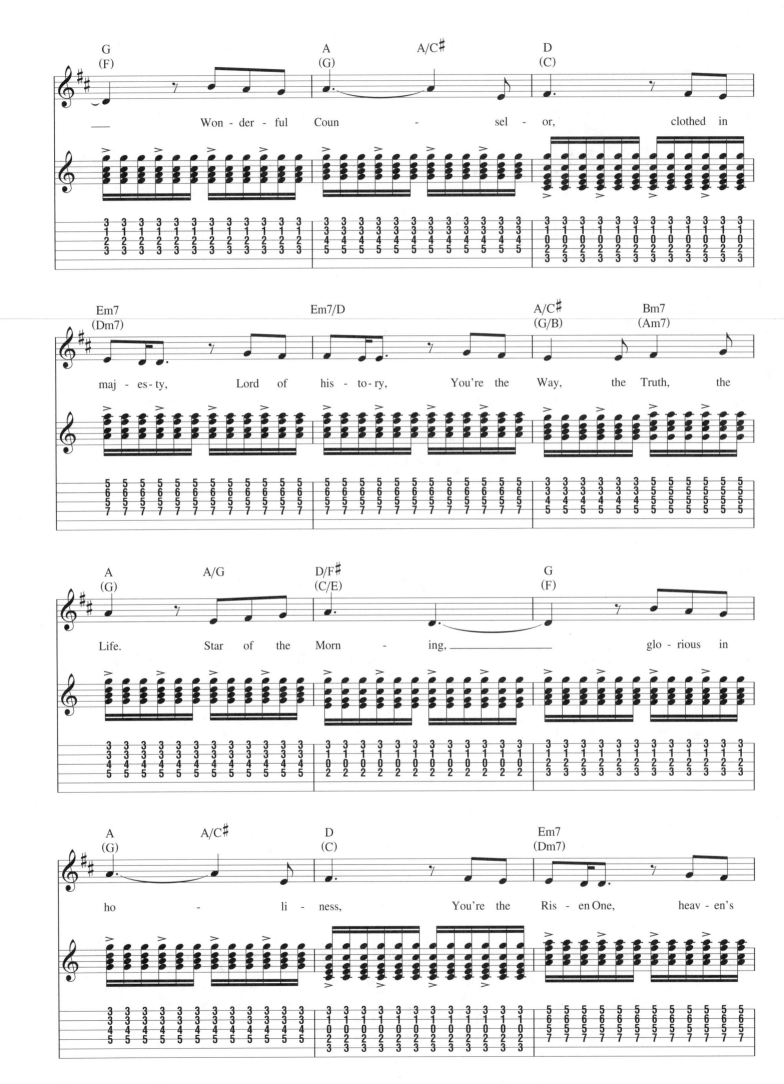

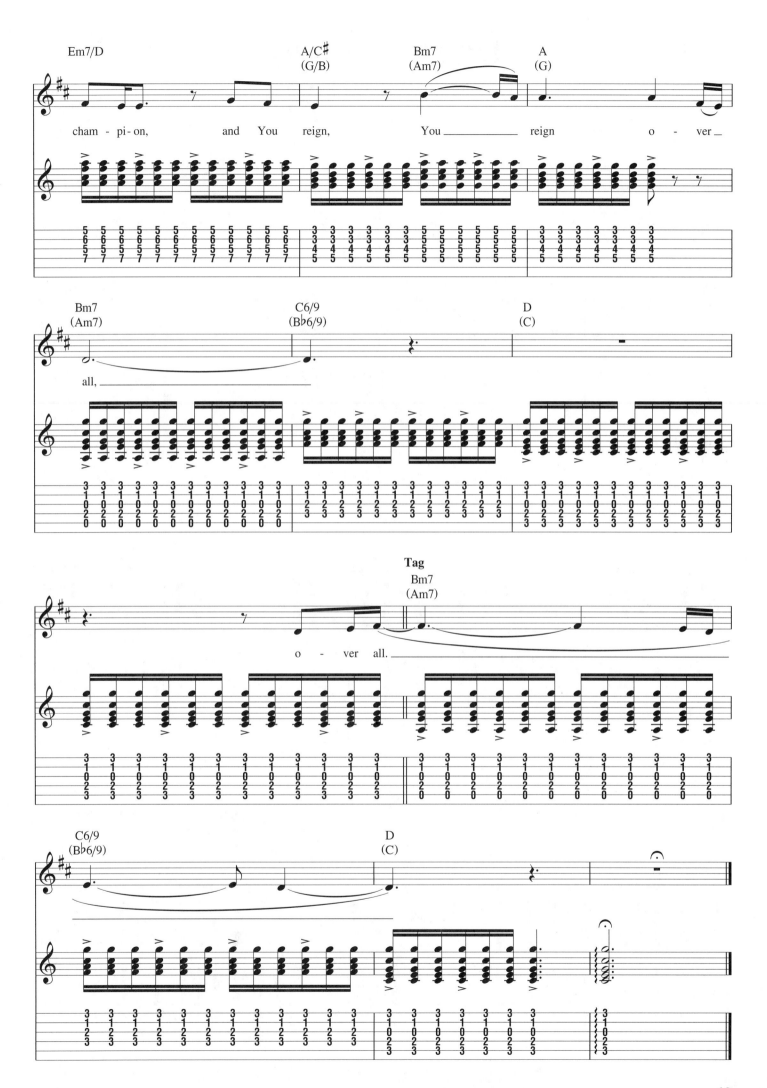

Days of Elijah

Words and Music by Robin Mark

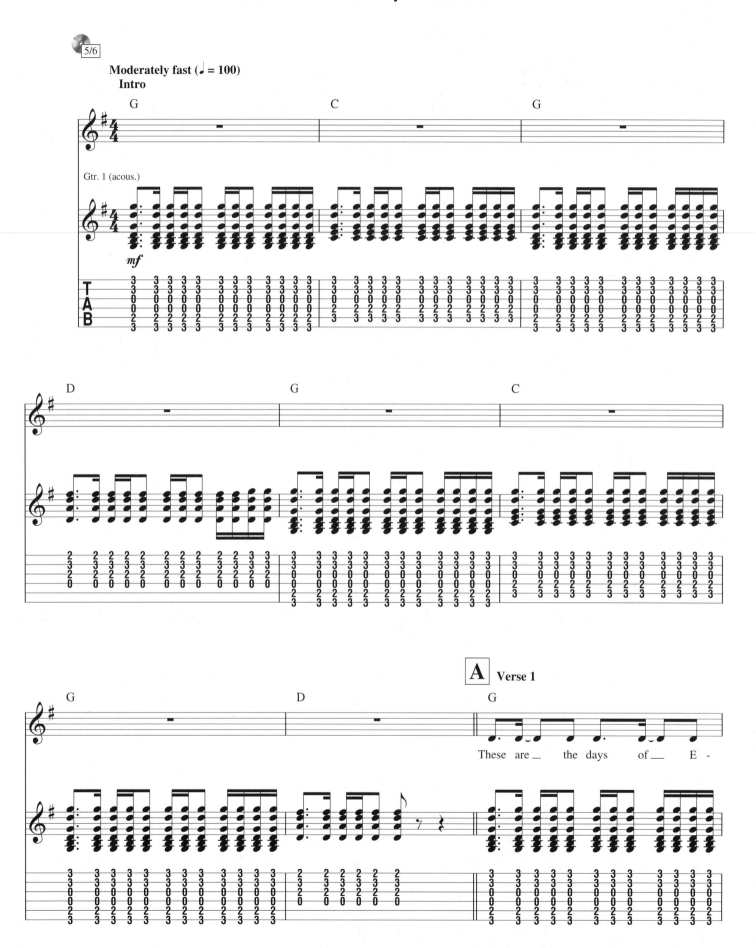

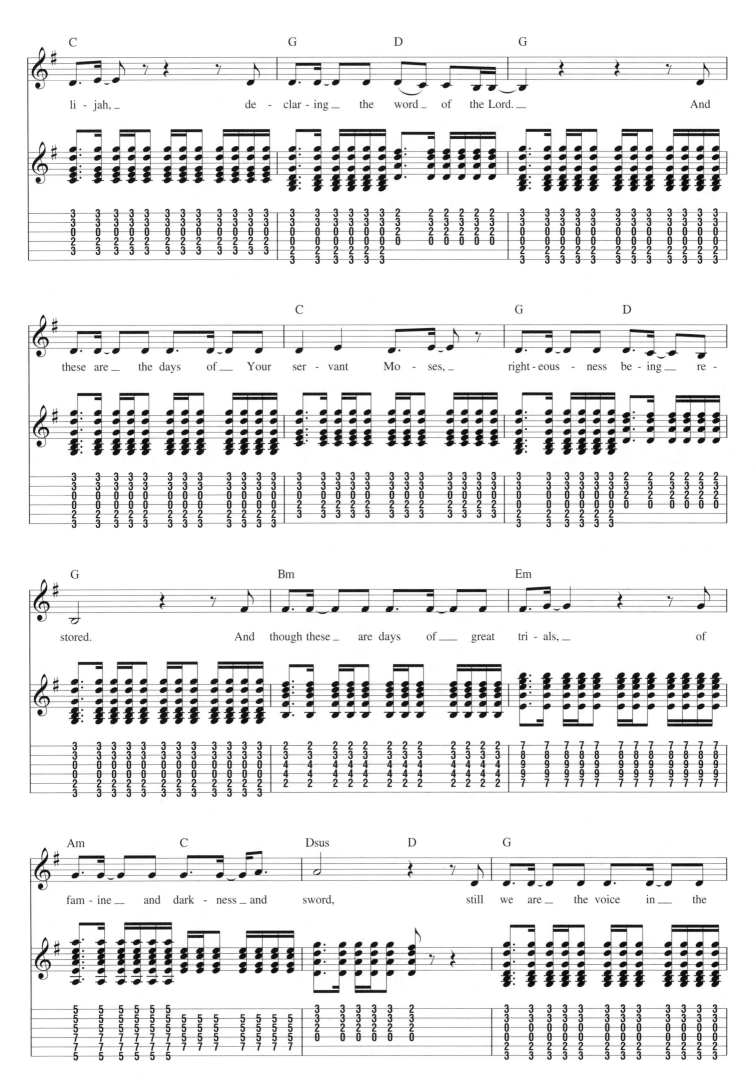

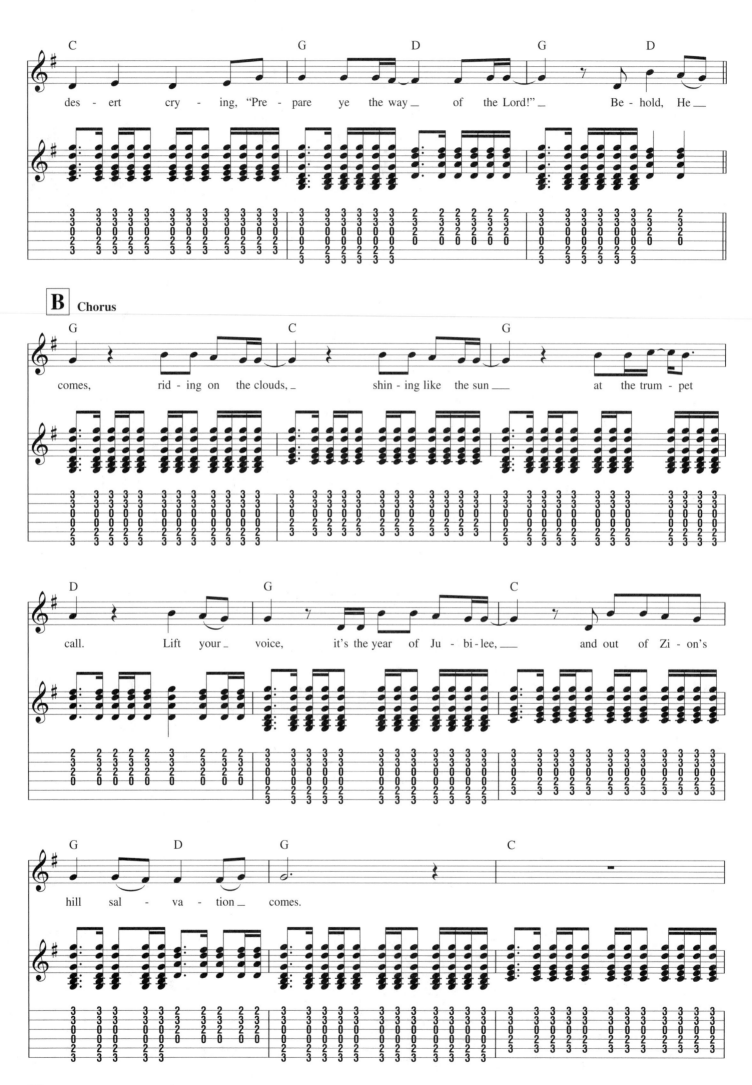

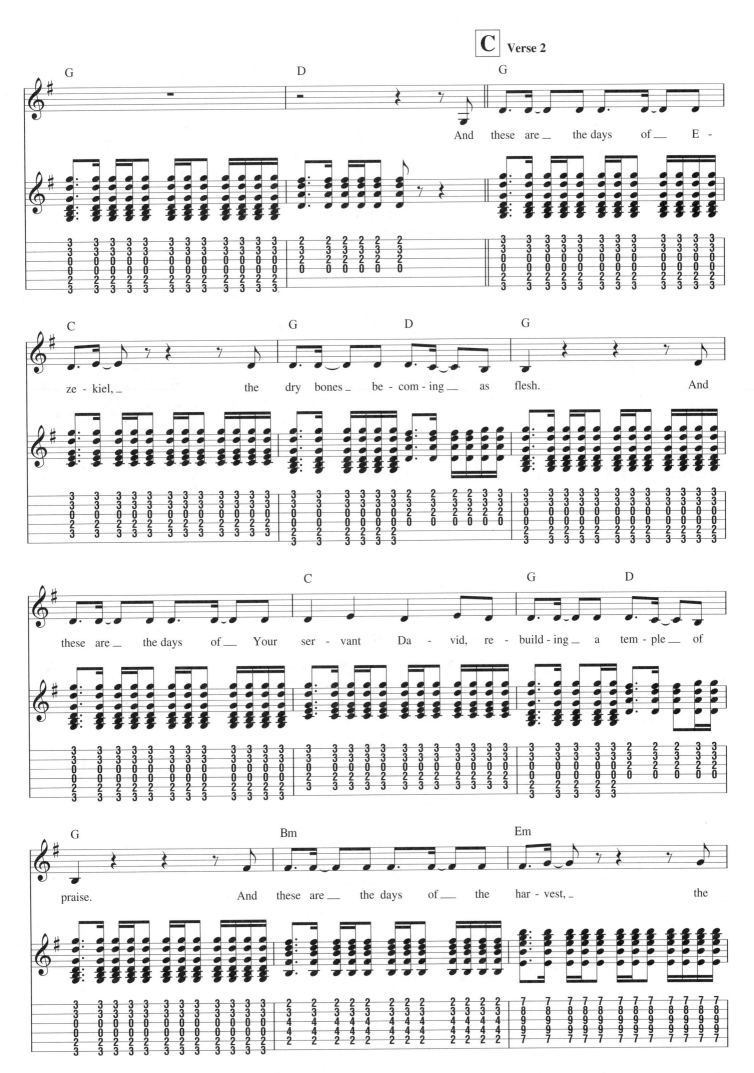

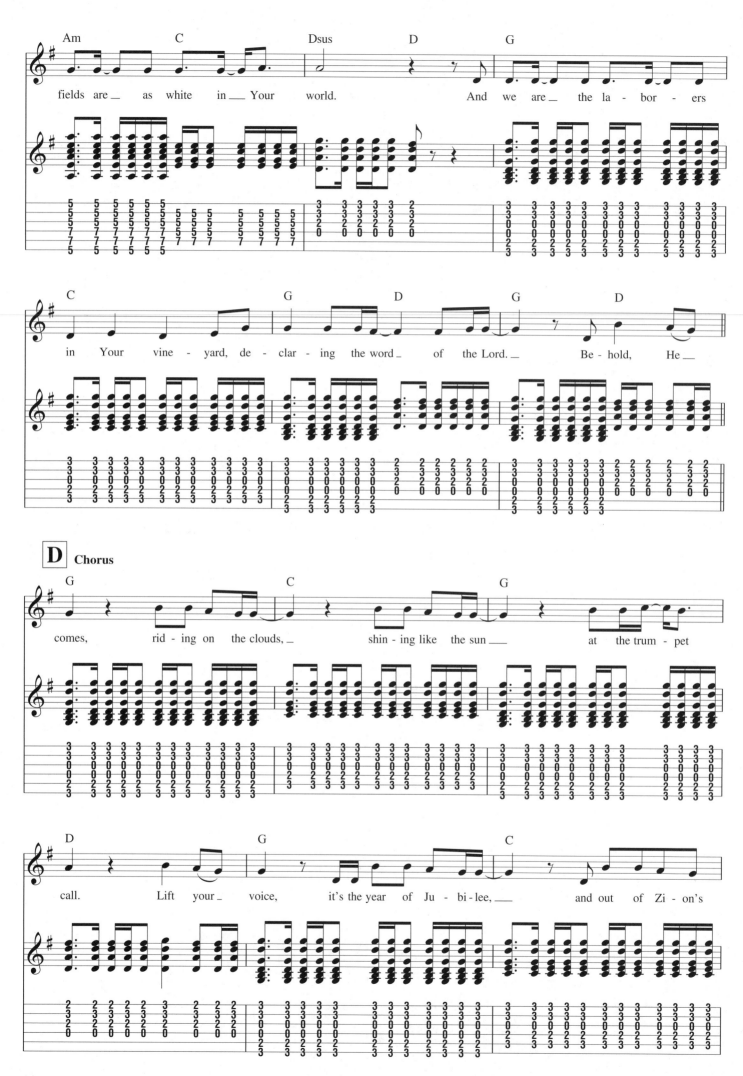

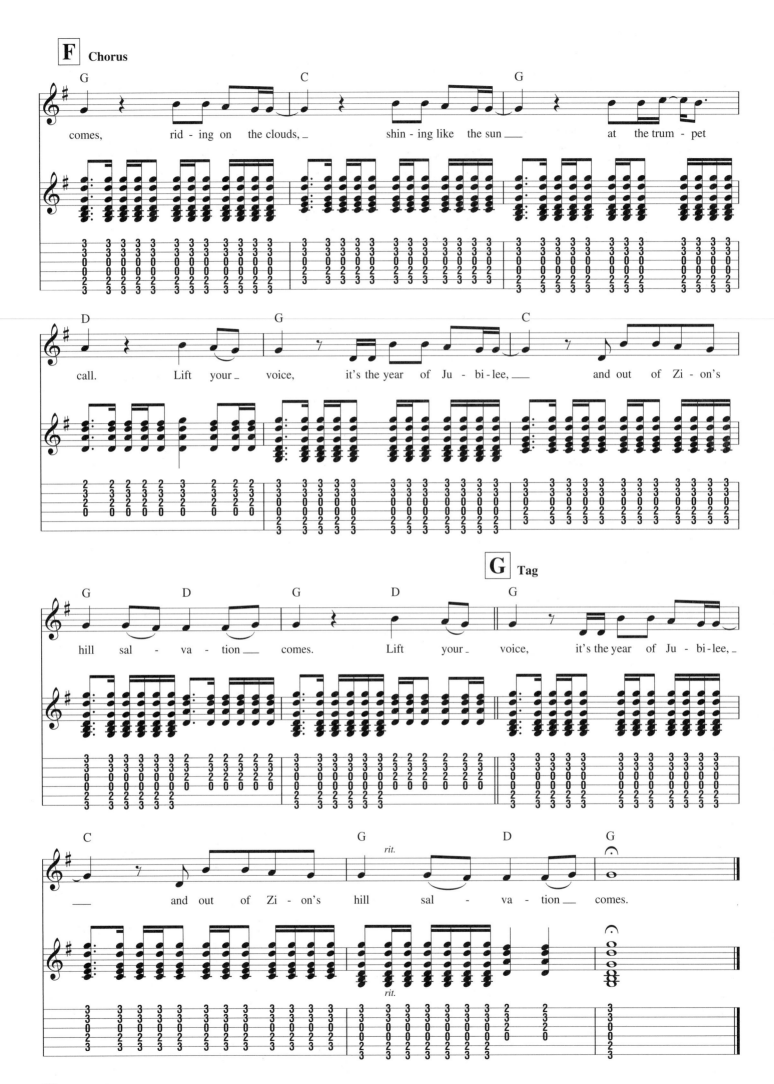

How Great Is Our God

Words and Music by Chris Tomlin, Jesse Reeves and Ed Cash

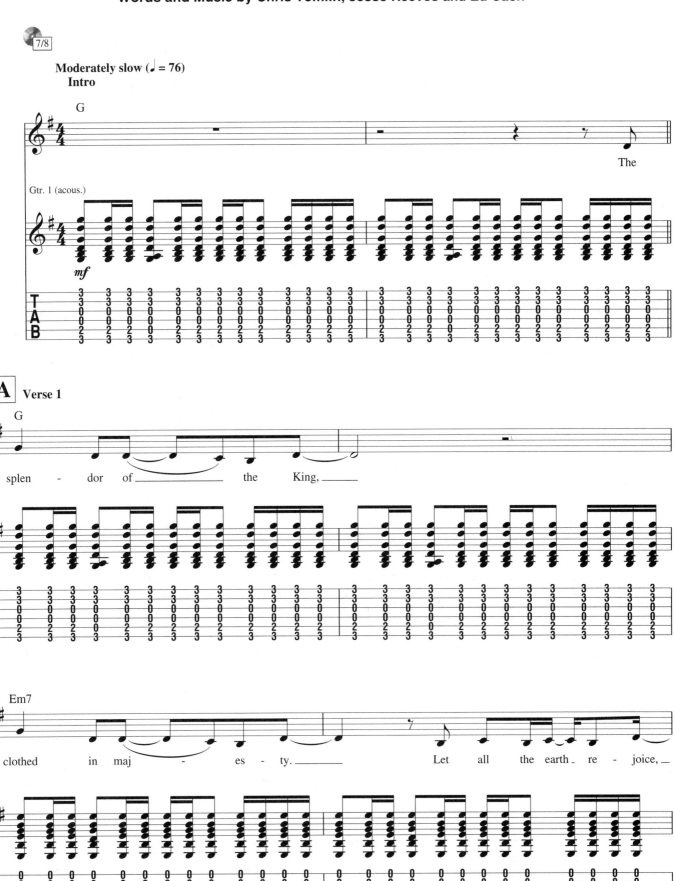

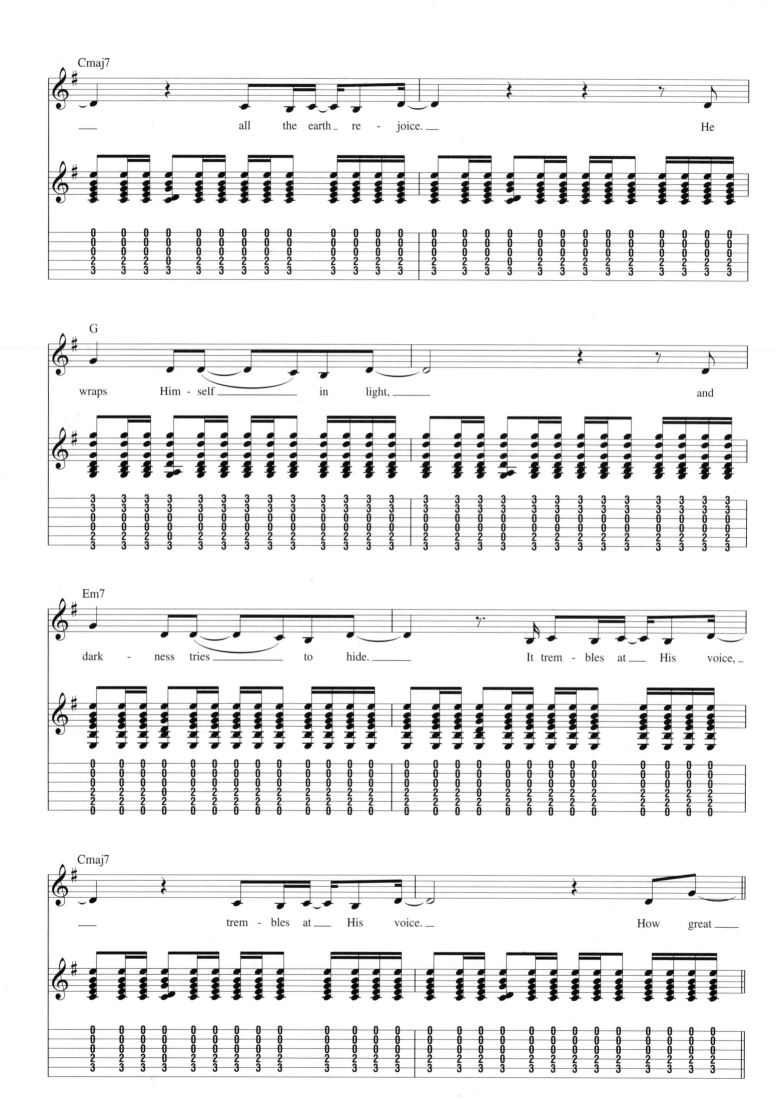

Chorus

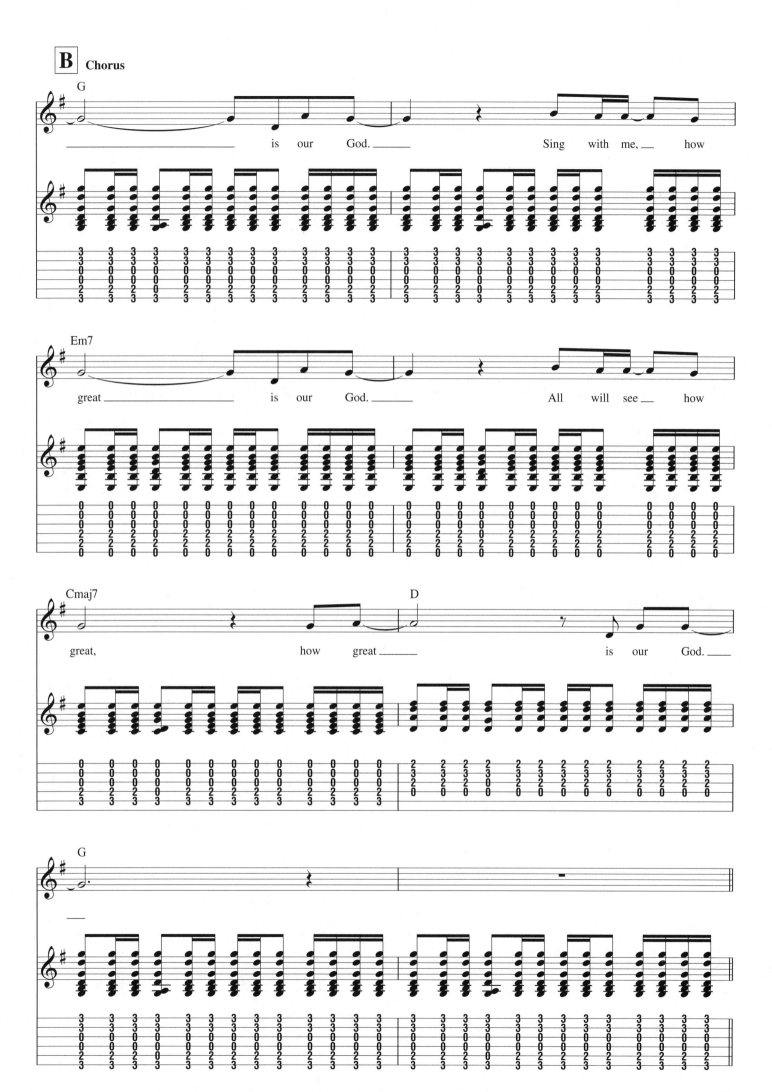

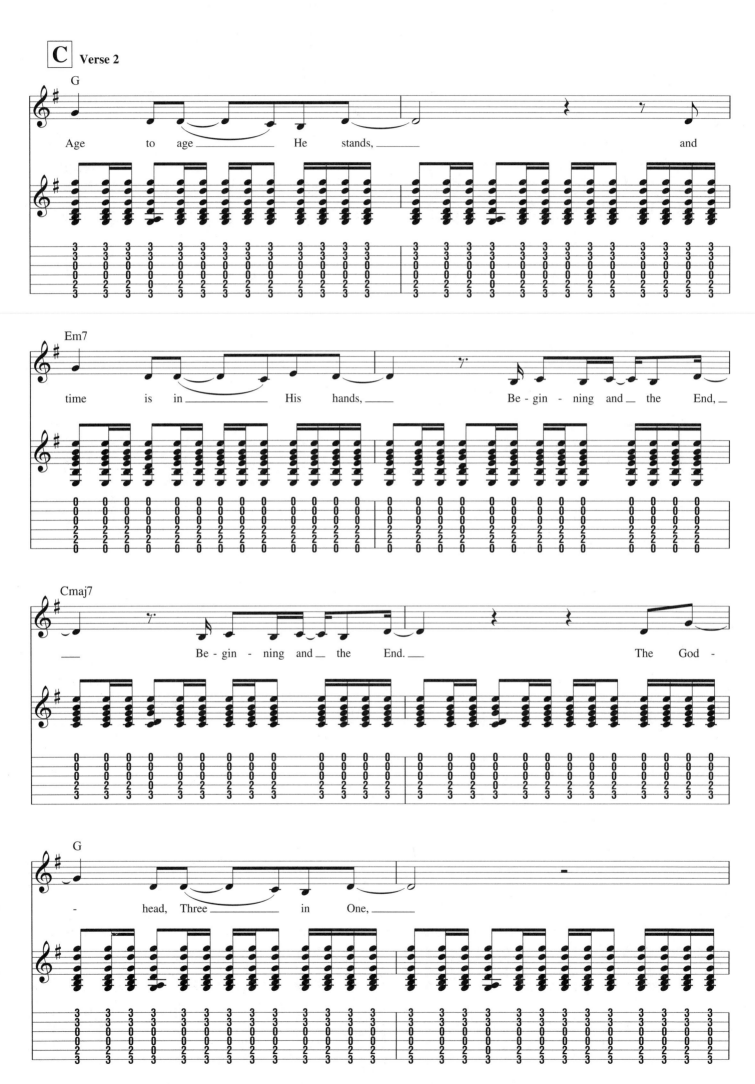

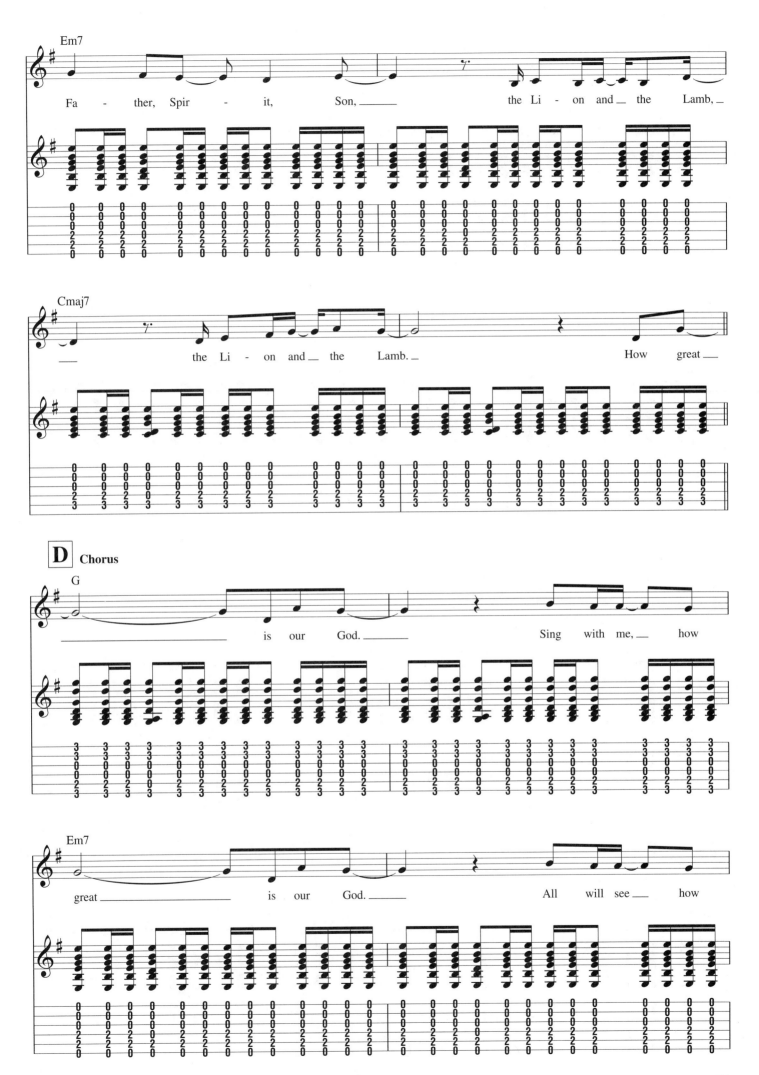

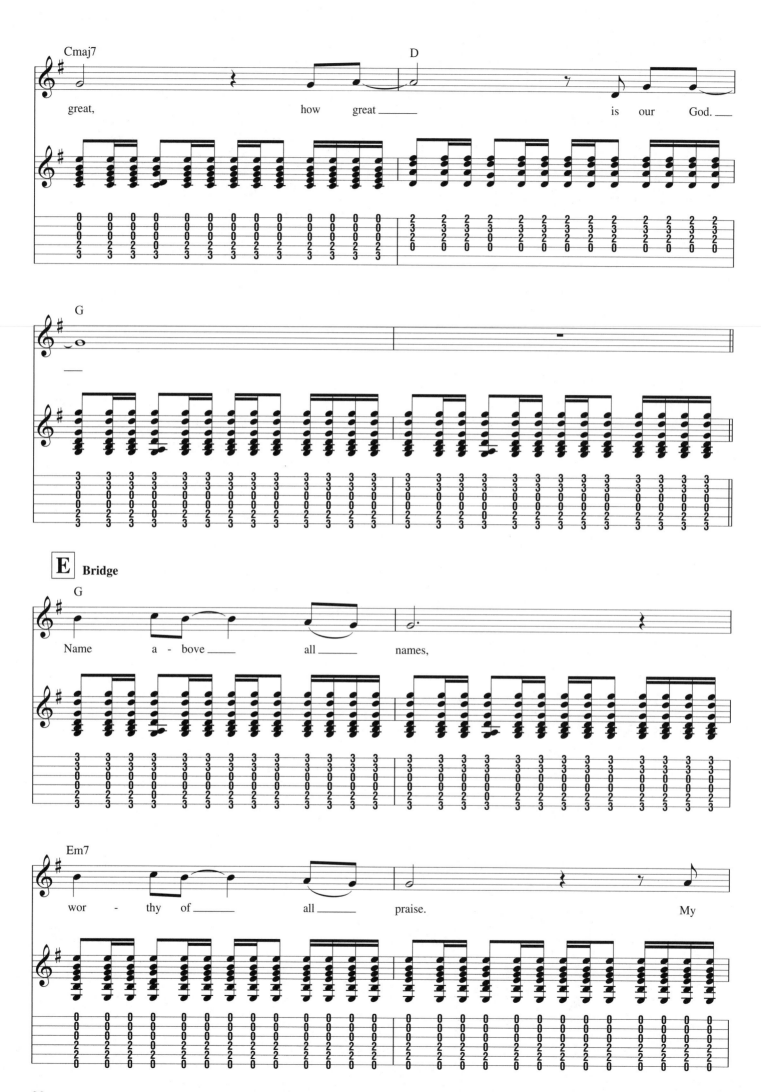

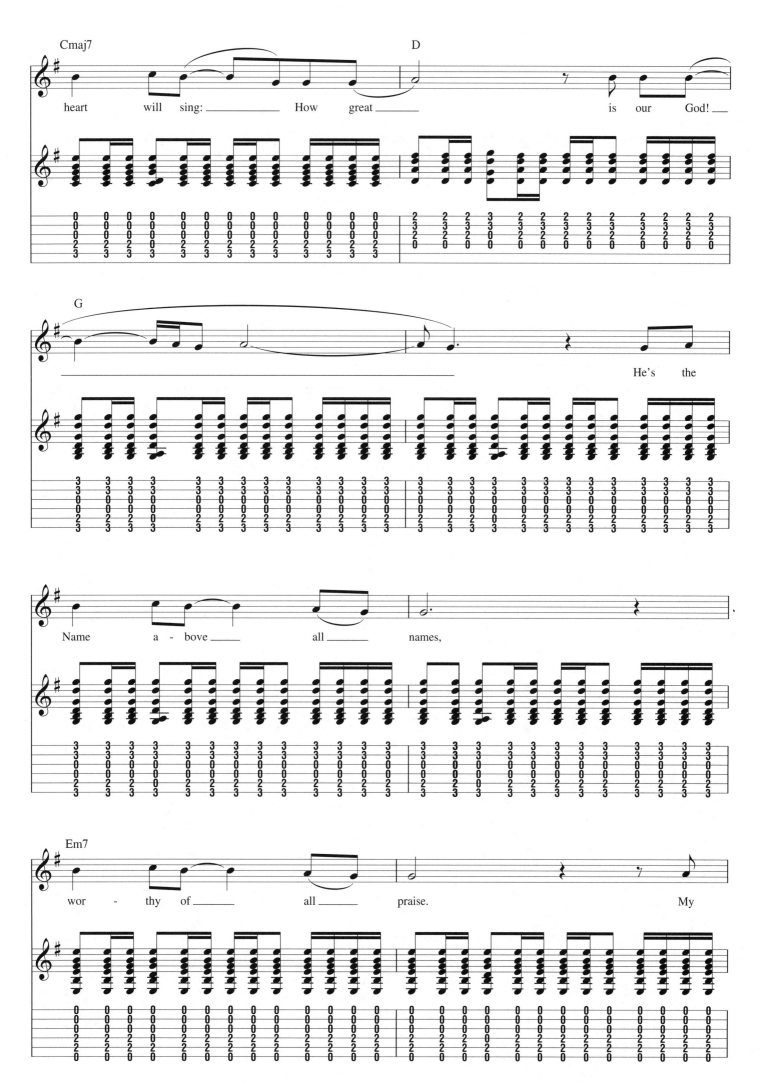

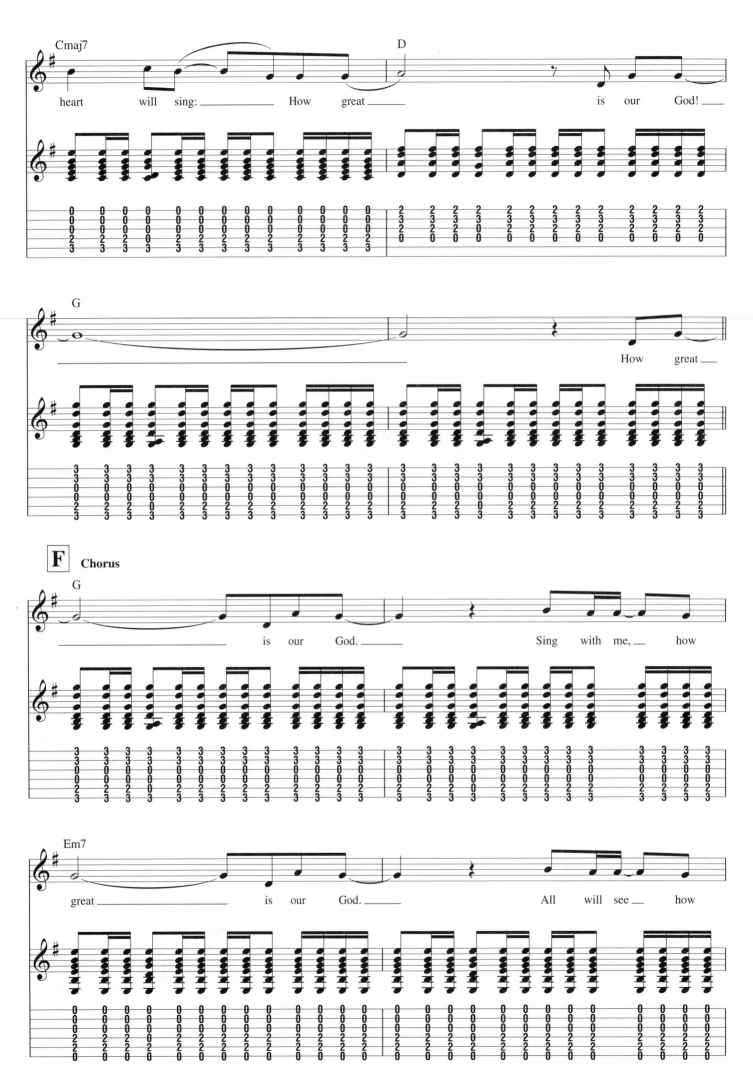

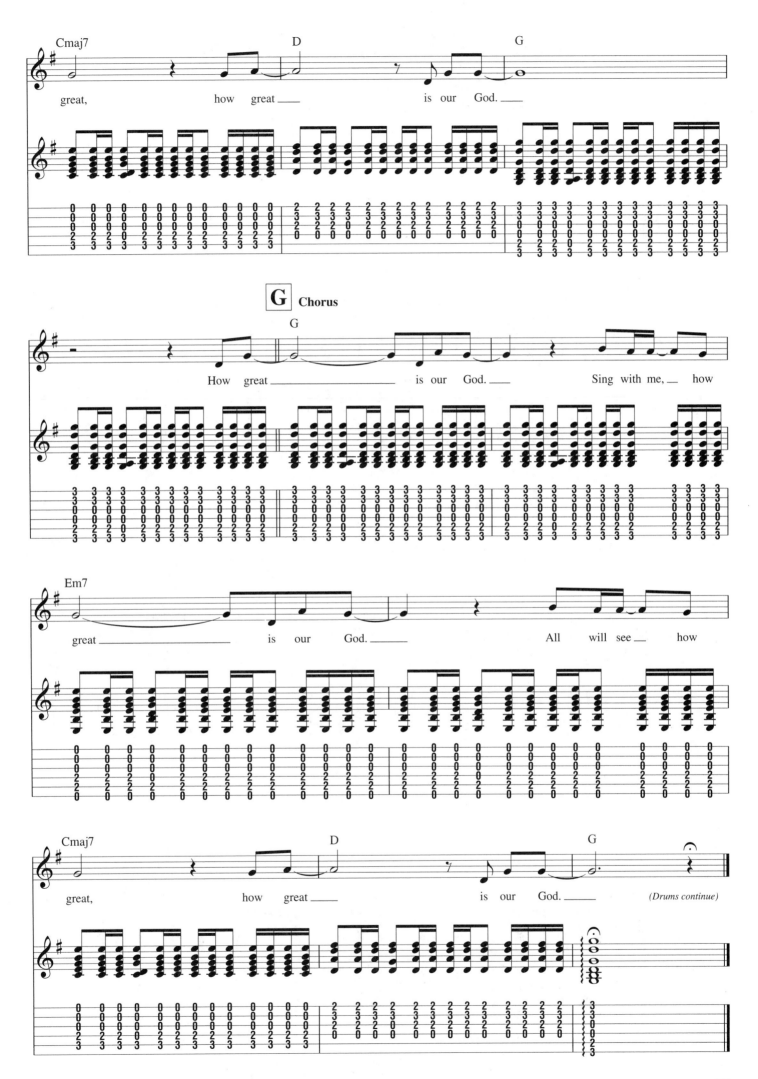

Let My Words Be Few
(I'll Stand in Awe of You)

Words and Music by Matt Redman and Beth Redman

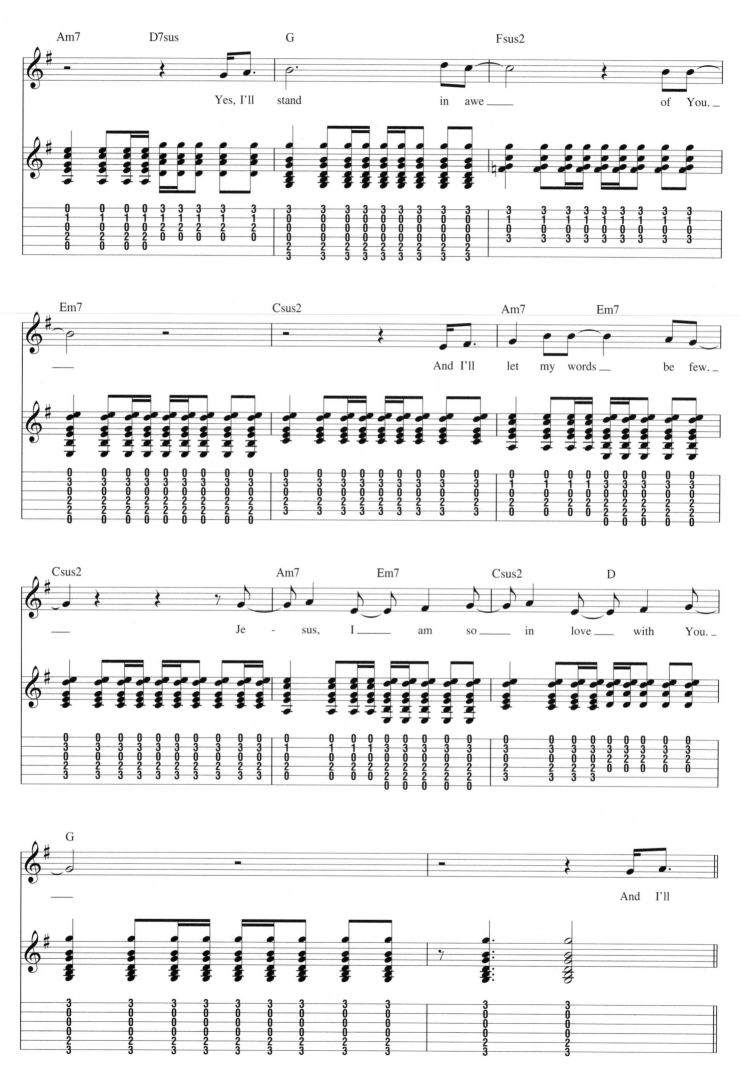

No One Like You

Words and Music by Jack Parker, Mike Dodson, Jason Solley, Mike Hogan, Jeremy Bush and David Crowder

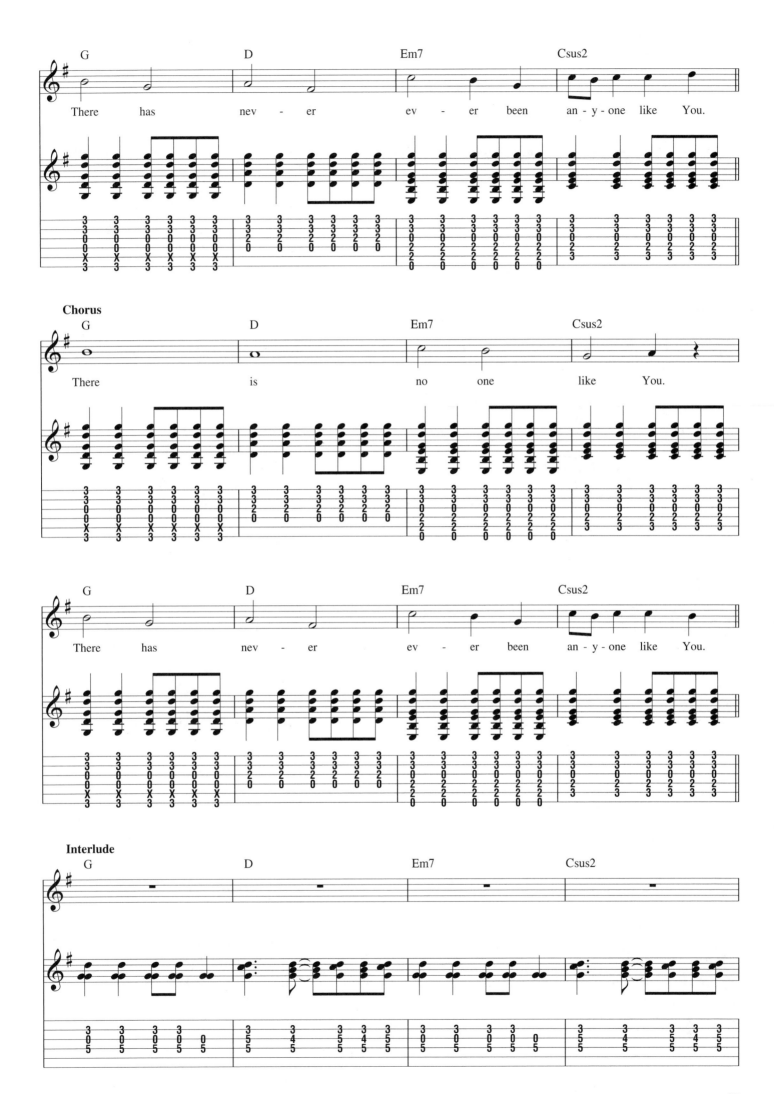

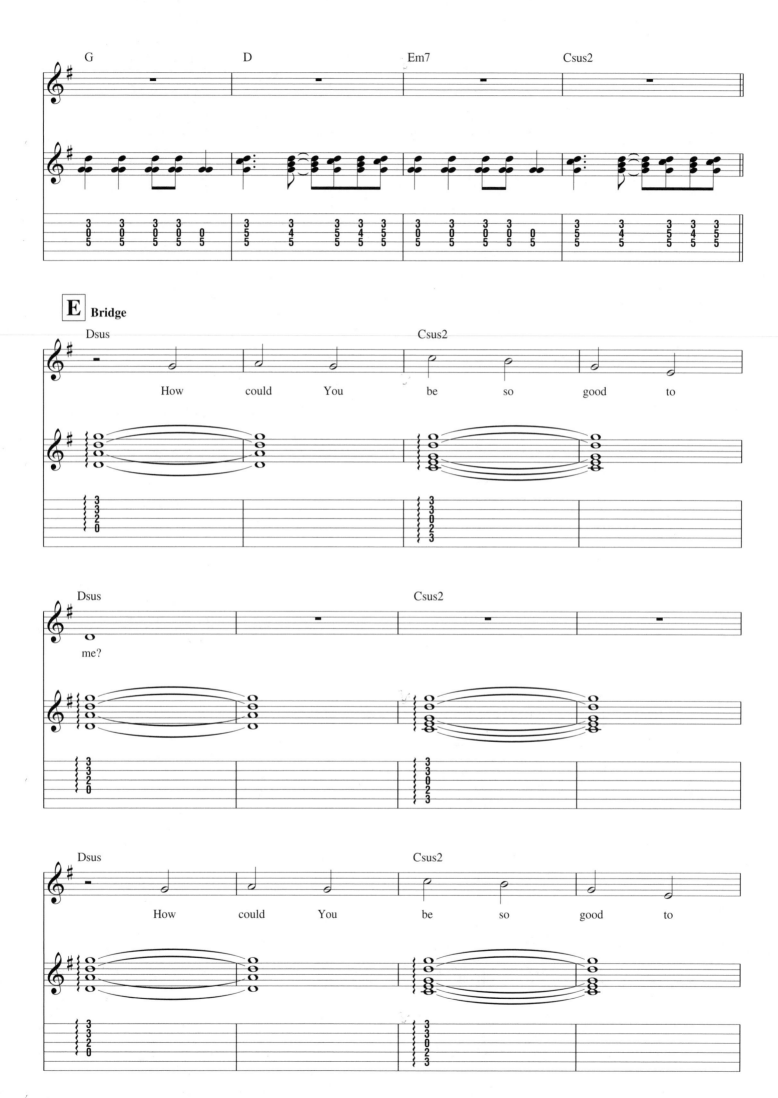

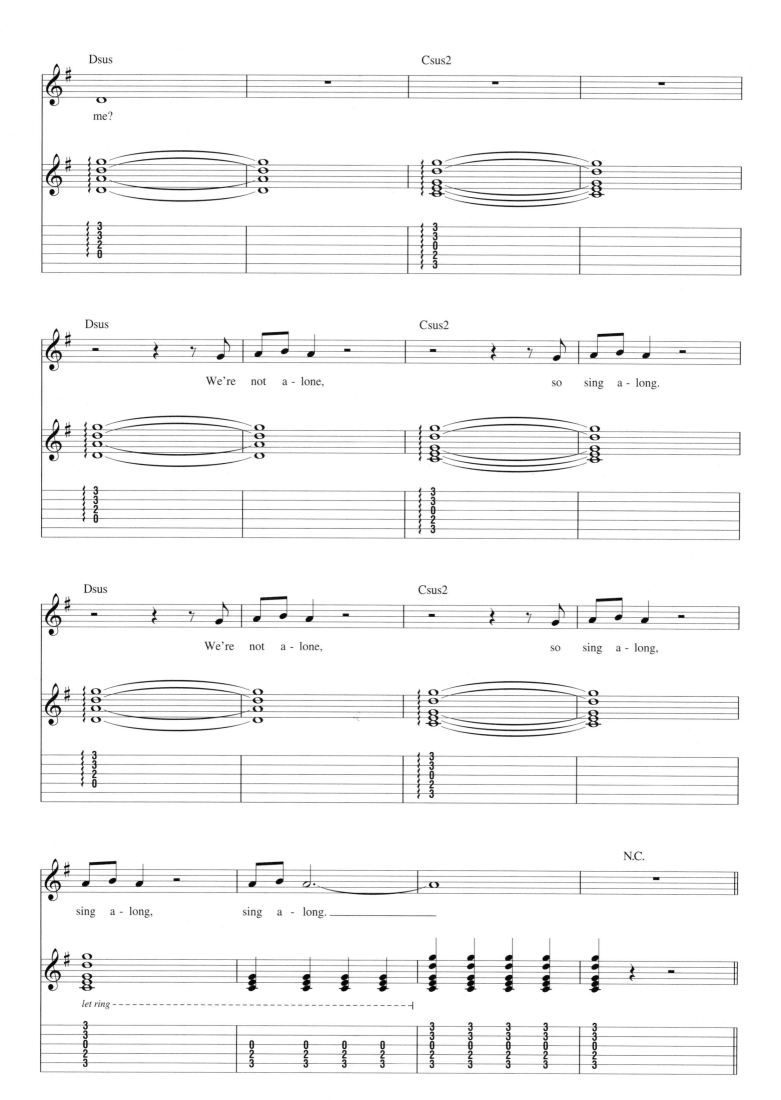

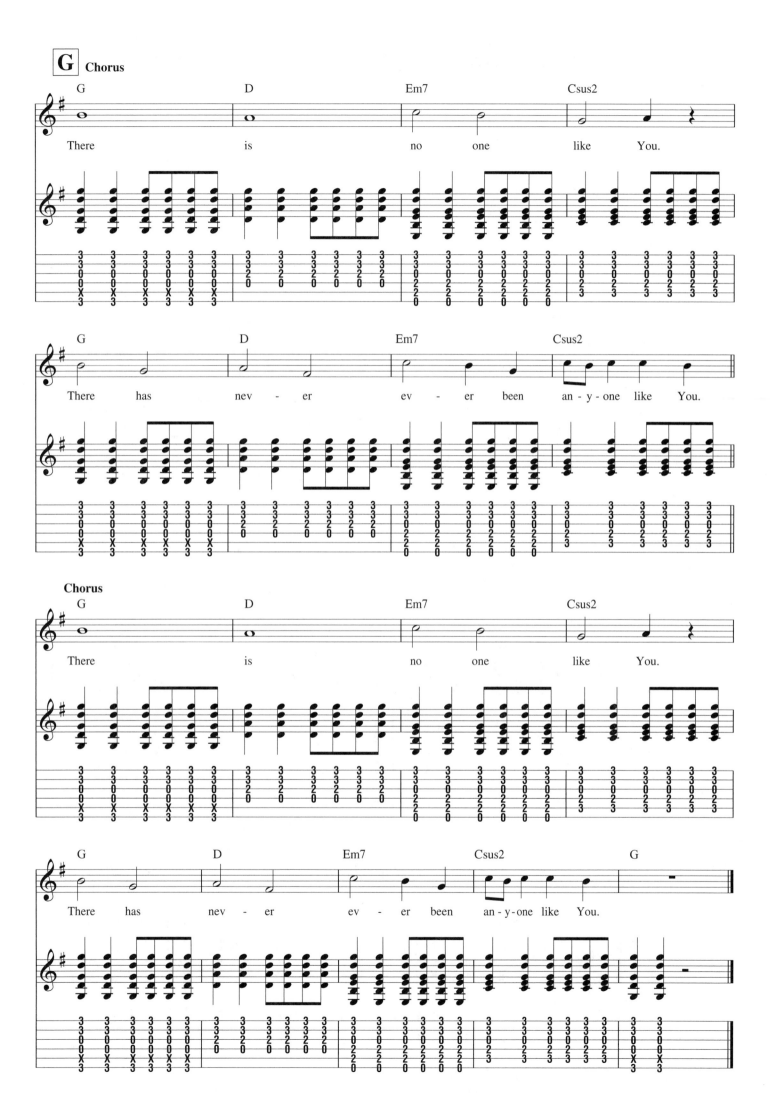

Yesterday, Today and Forever

Words and Music by Vicky Beeching

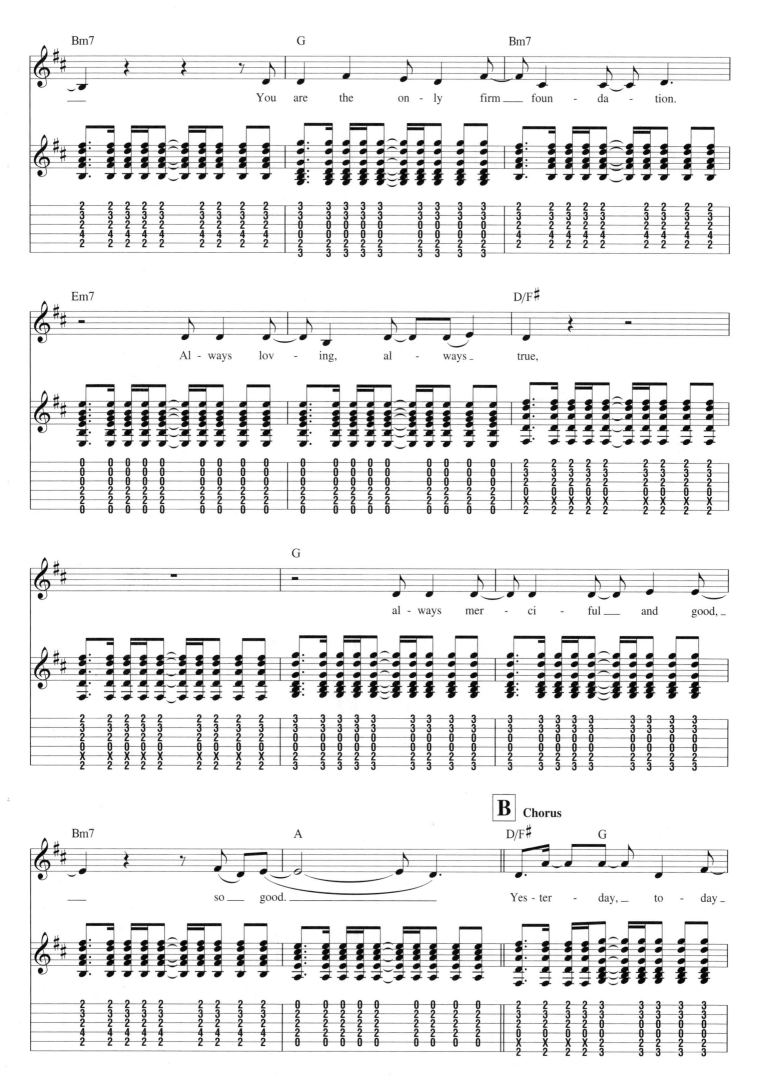

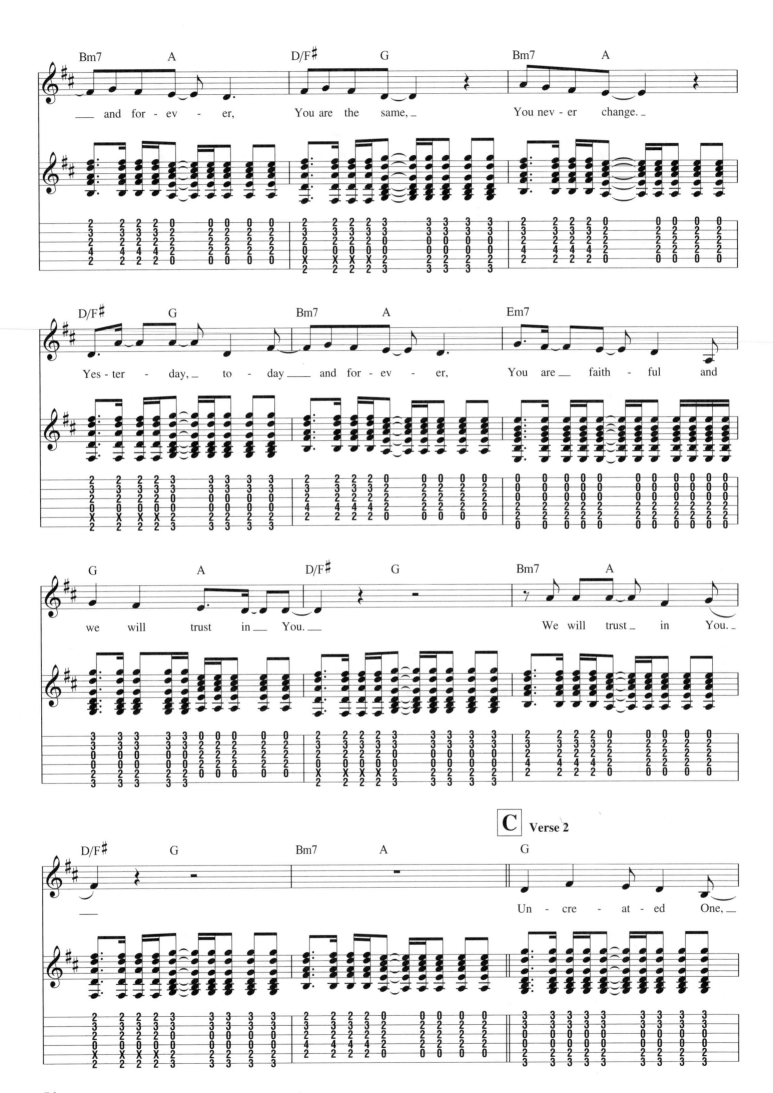

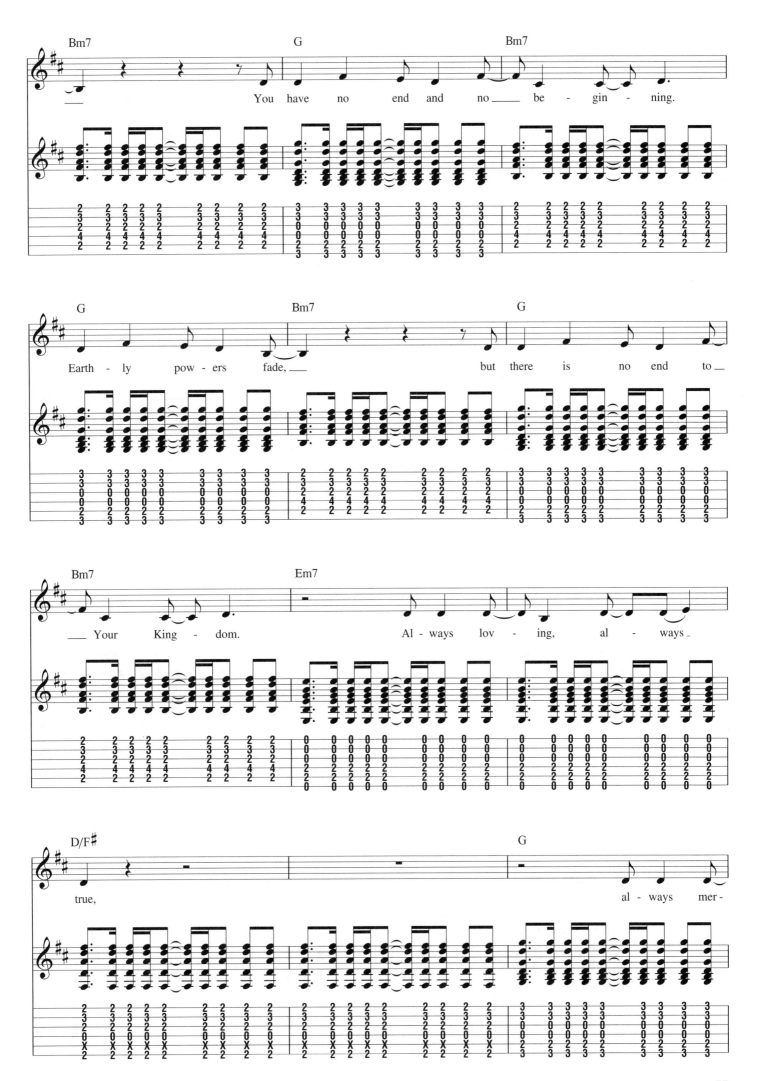

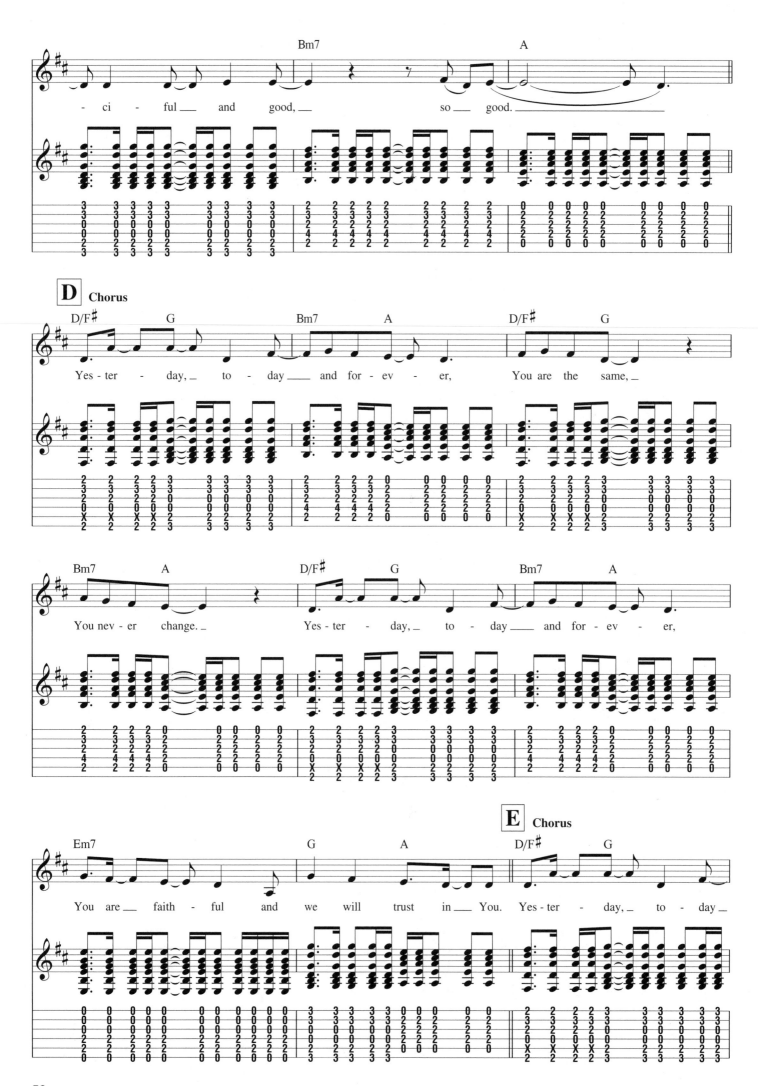

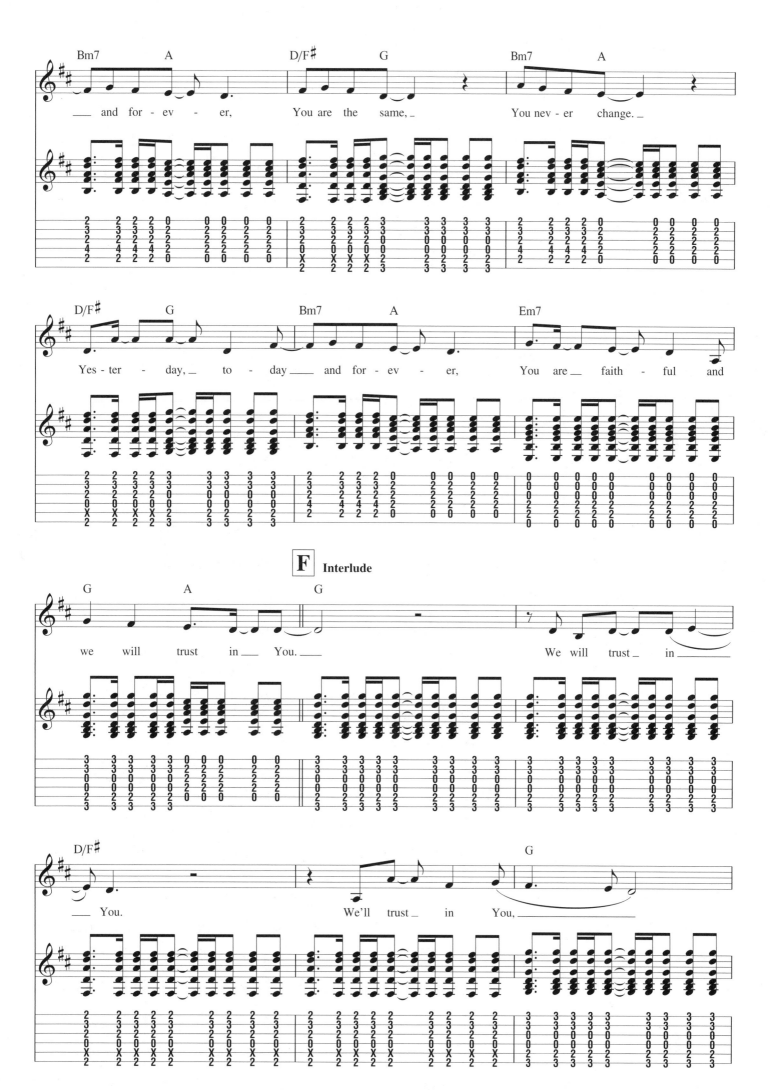

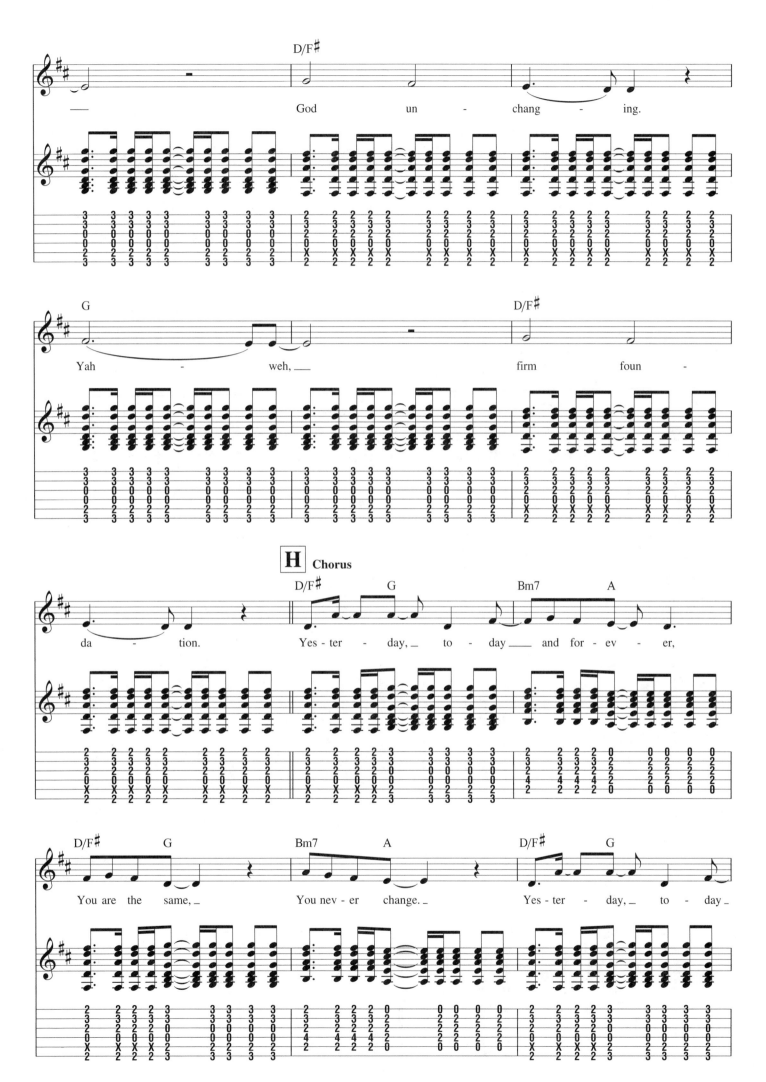

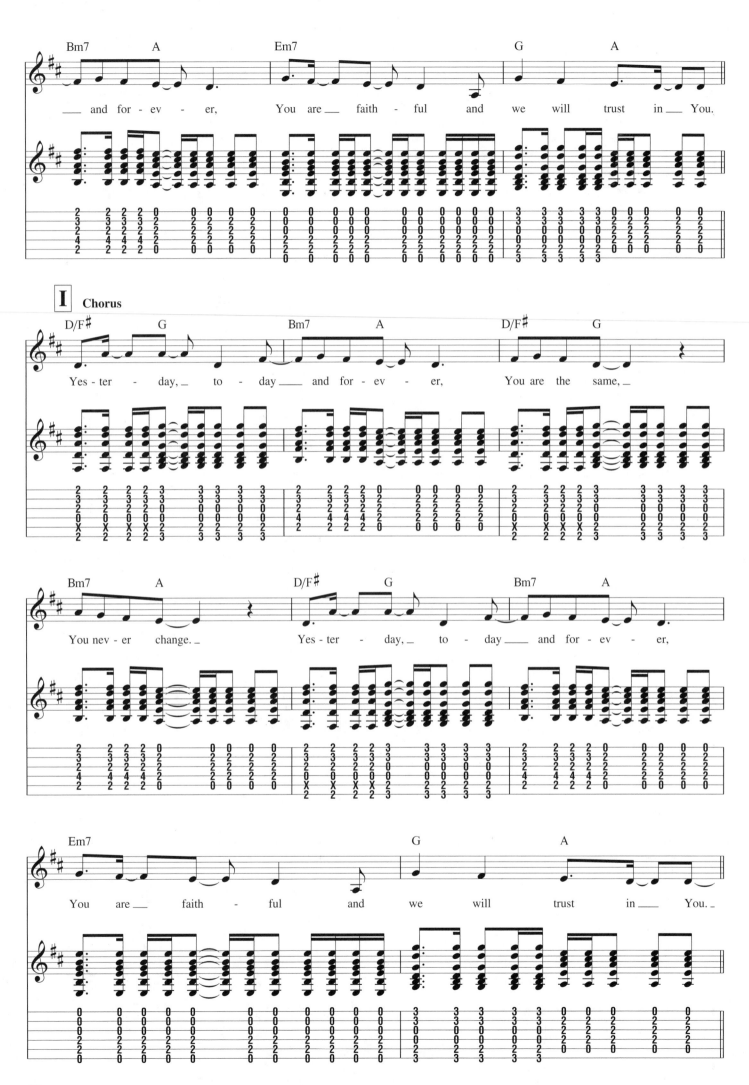

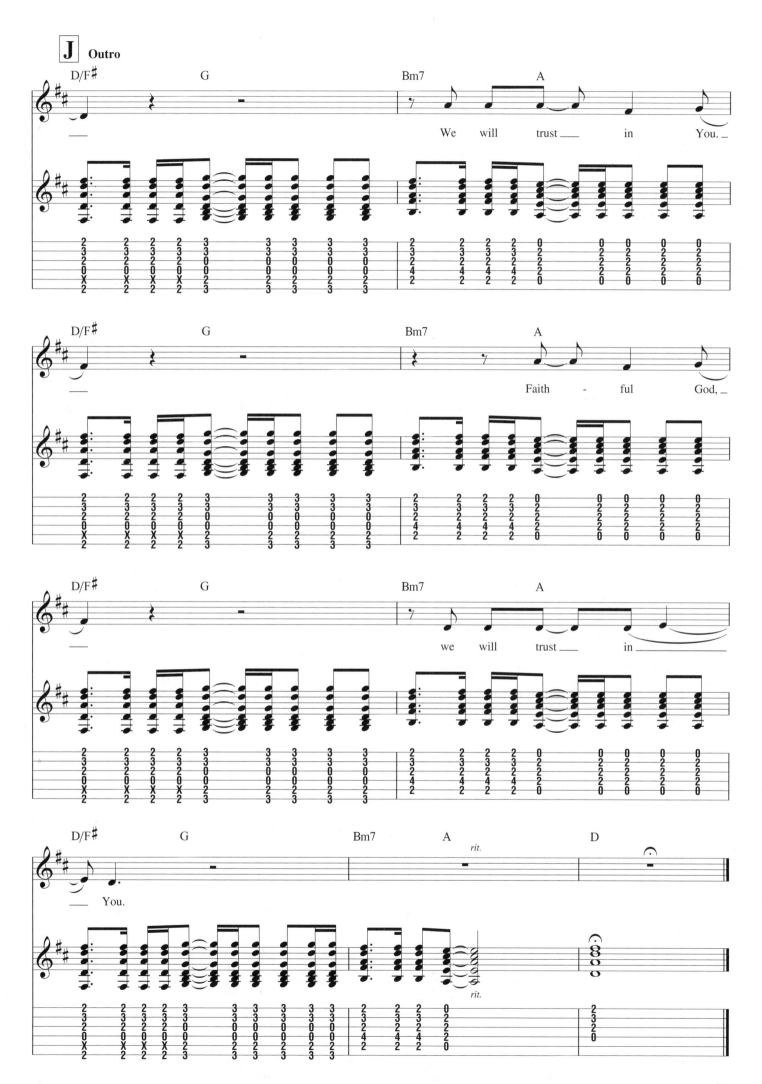

Wonderful Maker

Words and Music by Matt Redman and Chris Tomlin

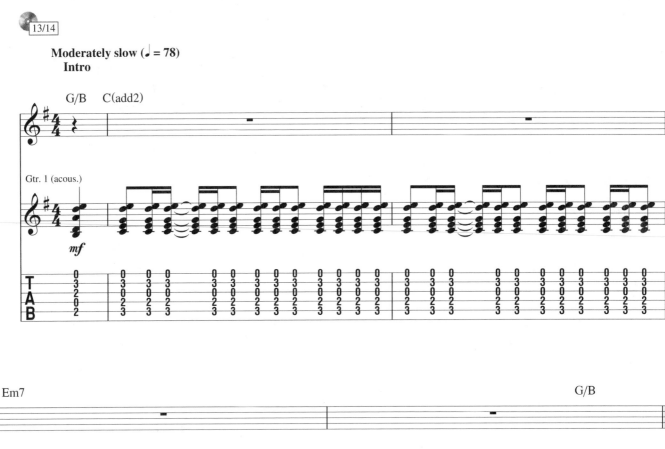

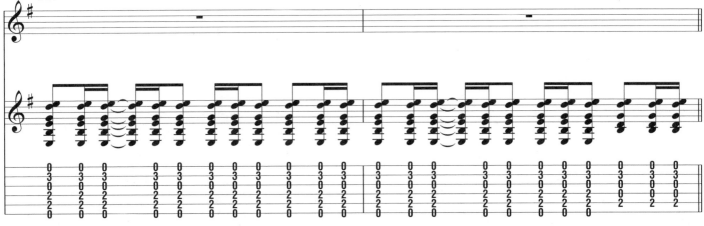

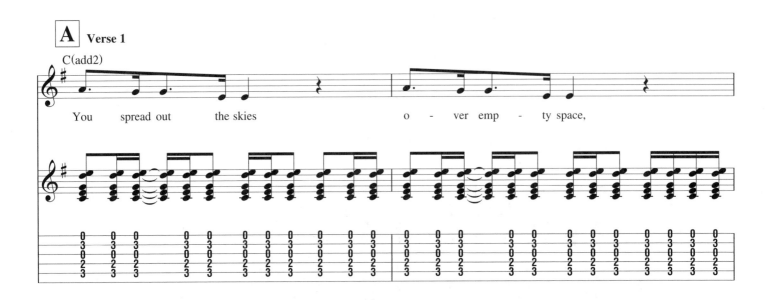

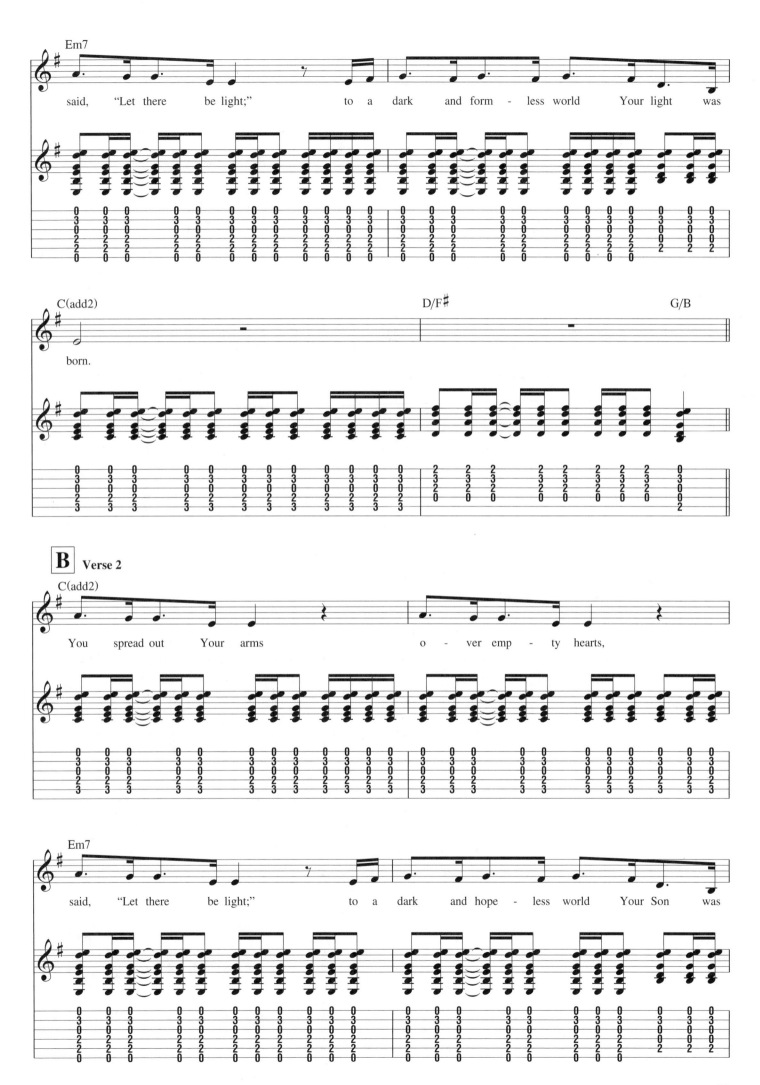

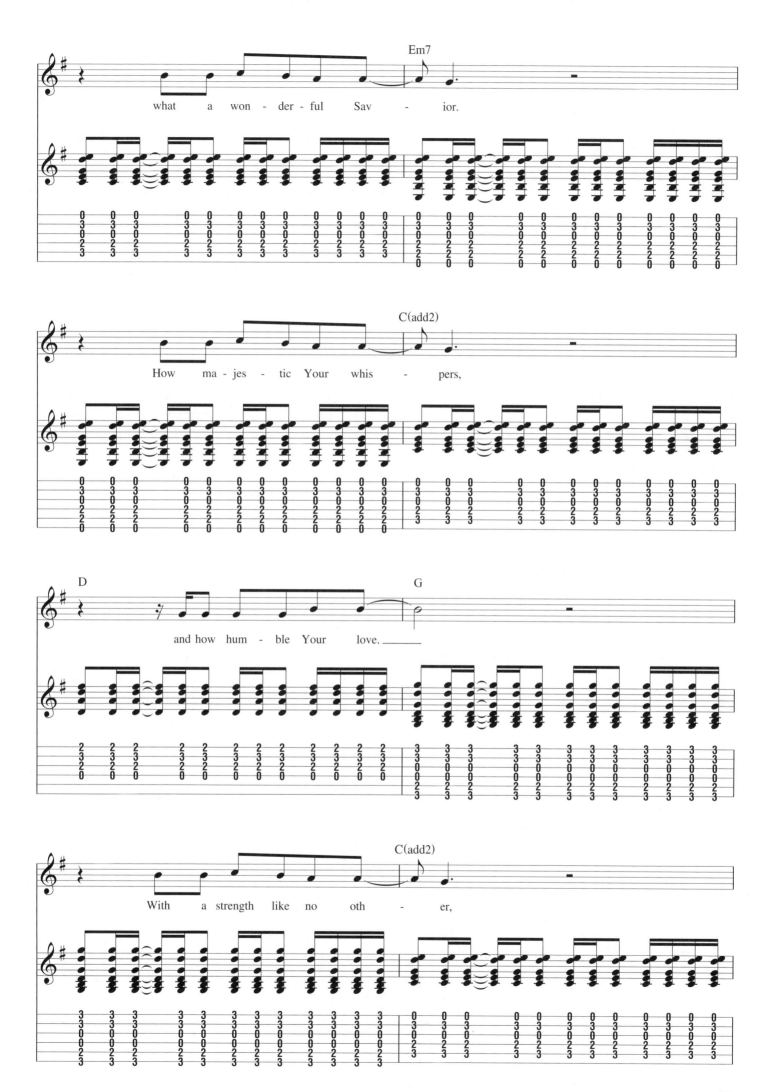

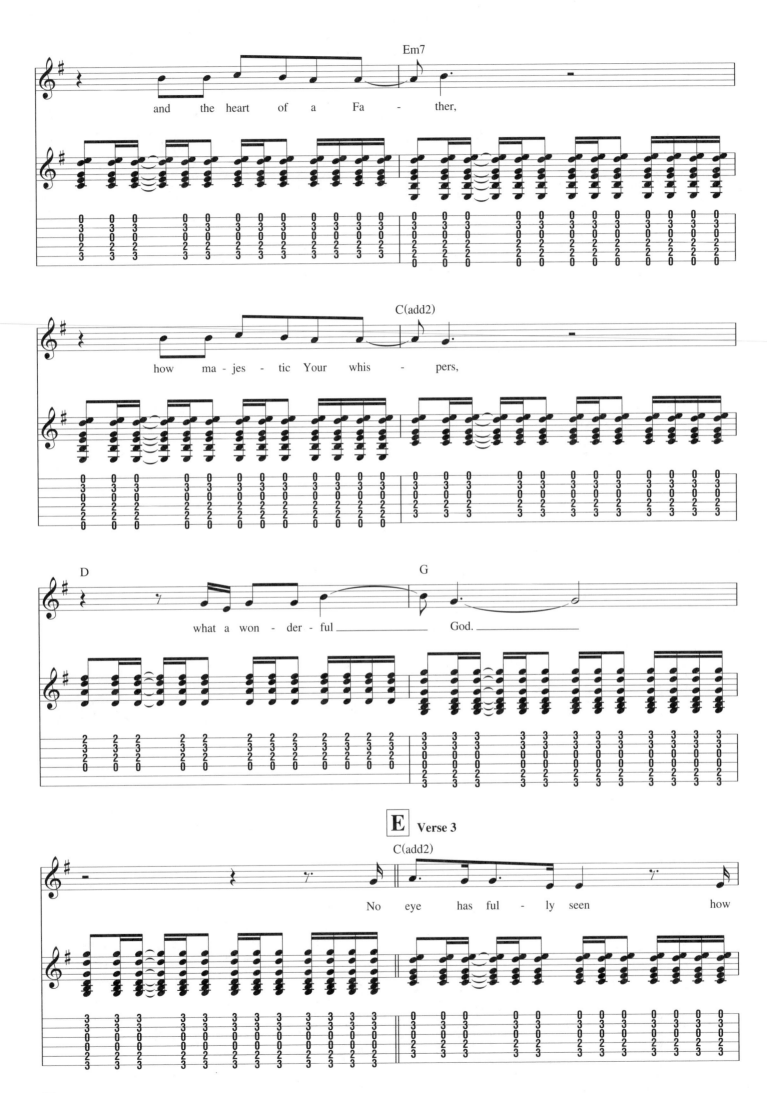

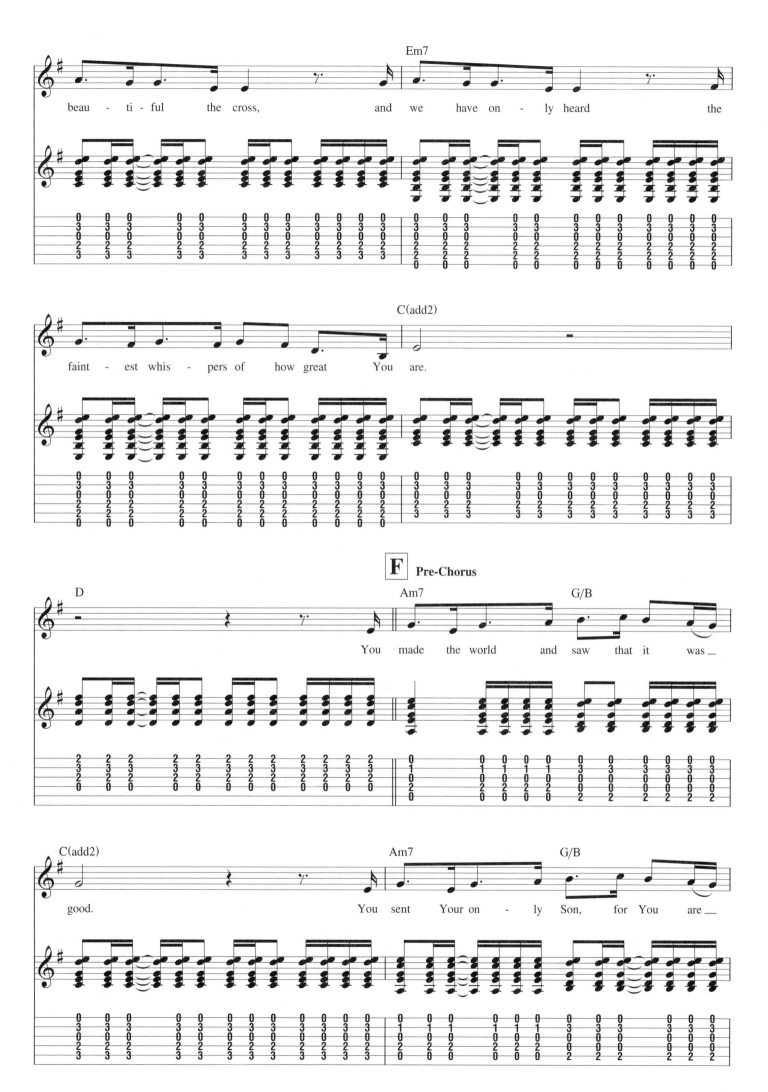

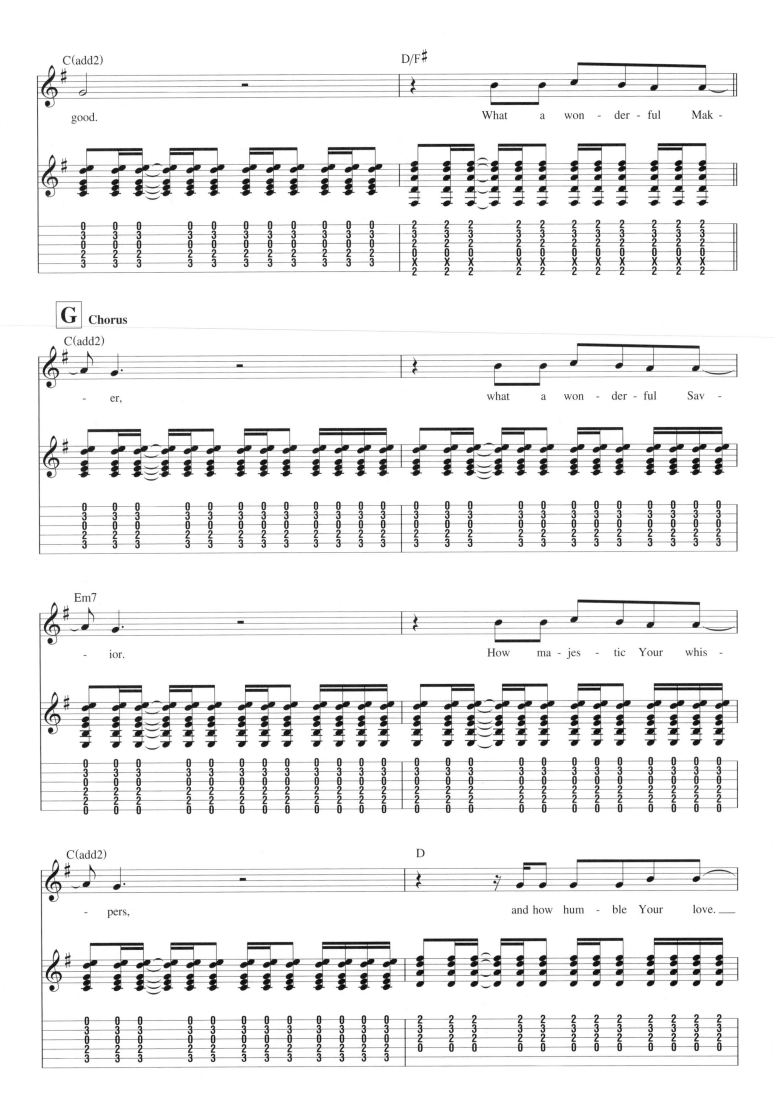

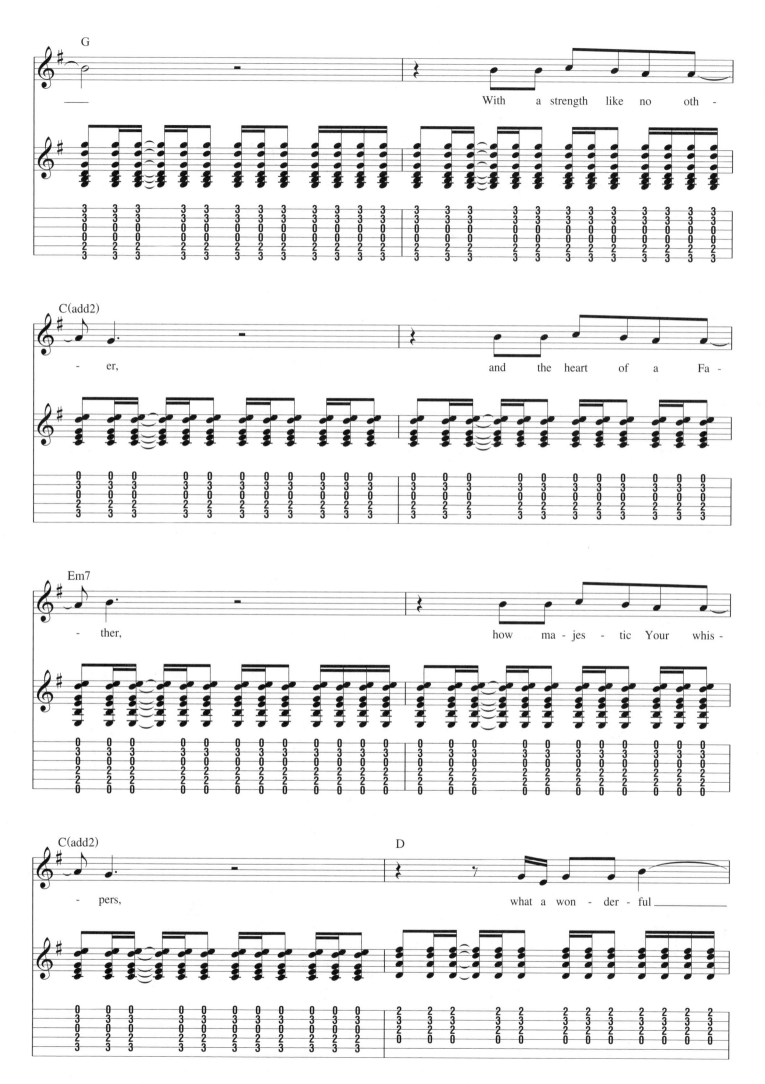

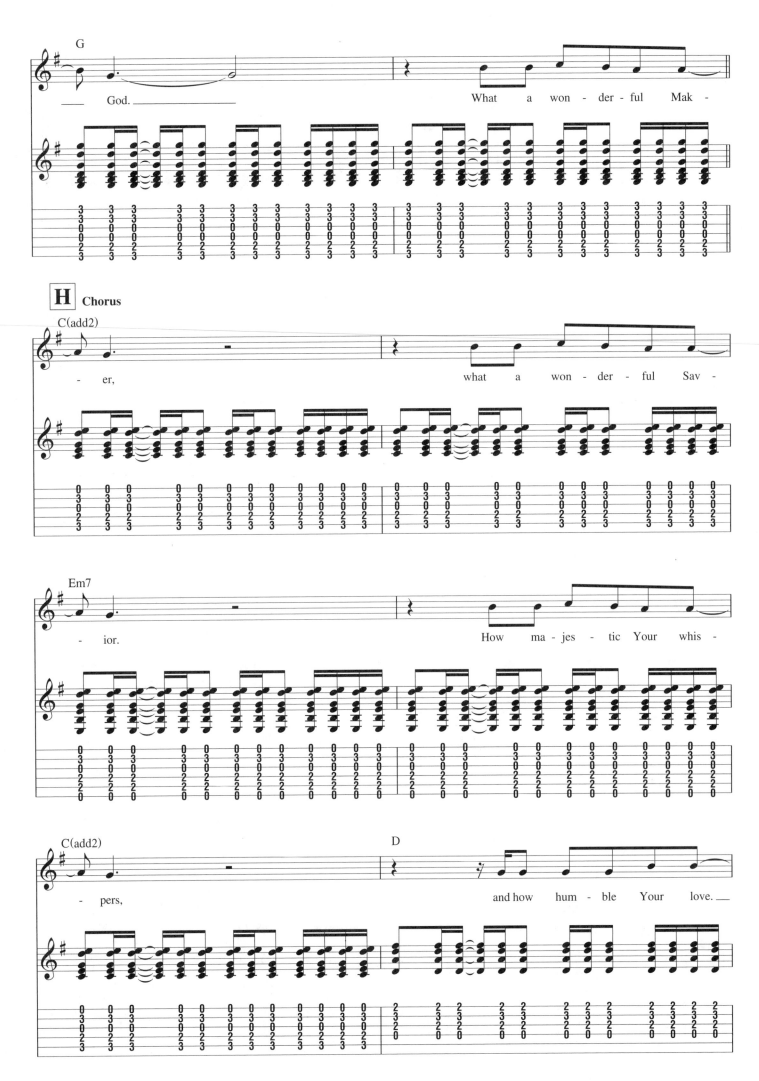

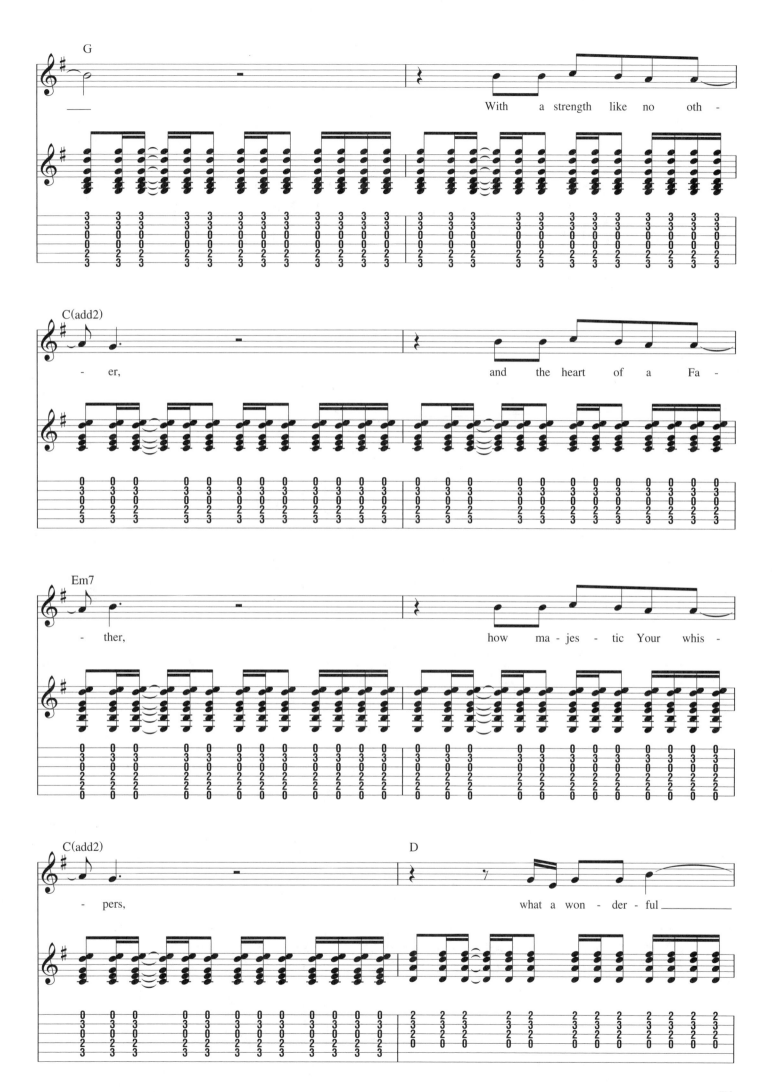

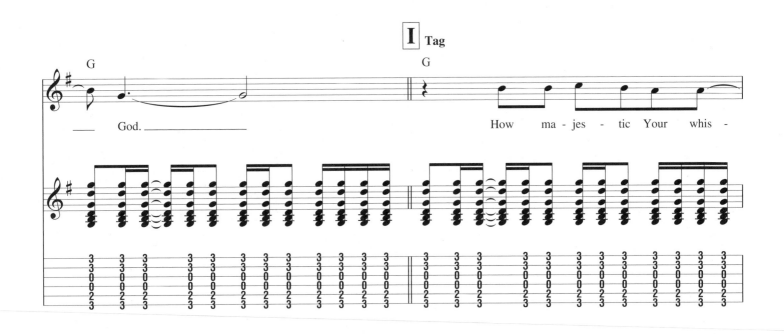

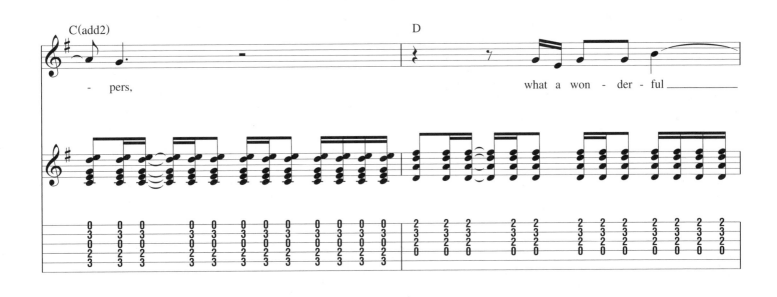

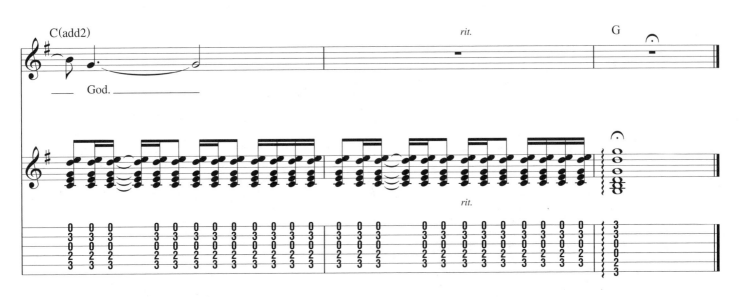

ABOVE ALL

PAUL BALOCHE and LENNY LeBLANC

Key of **G Major, 4/4**

INTRO:

G   G/B   C   D   Em7   D   C   Dsus   D

VERSE:

```
        C      Dsus        G
Above all powers,     above all kings
        C        Dsus     G
Above all nature and all created things
        Em         G/D          C    G/B
Above all wisdom and all the ways of man
Am7                          Dsus   D
You were here before the world began
        C      Dsus        G
Above all kingdoms,     above all thrones
        C      Dsus        G
Above all wonders the world has ever known
        Em       G/D          C    G/B
Above all wealth and treasures of the earth
Am7                              B7
There's no way to measure what You're worth
```

CHORUS:

```
G   Am7   D        G
Crucified,   laid behind a stone
   G    Am7   D       G
You lived to die   rejected and alone
    Em    G/D          C    G/B
Like a rose trampled on the ground
        Am7  G/B          C   Dsus
You took the fall     and thought of me
        G   G/B  C  Dsus  D
Above all   (C/E  D/F♯)
```

(REPEAT VERSE)

(REPEAT CHORUS 2X)

TAG:

```
D/F♯  Em  G/D          C    G/B
Like a rose trampled on the ground
        Am7  G/B          C   Dsus
You took the fall     and thought of me
        G   G/B  C  Dsus  D  G (hold)
Above all
```

BEAUTIFUL SAVIOR (ALL MY DAYS)

STUART TOWNEND

Key of **D Major**, 6/8

CAPO II (C MAJOR)
Chord symbols represent overall harmony for capoed guitar.
See page 10 for actual sounding chords.

INTRO (2X):

Am7   B♭6/9   C (2 bars)

VERSE 1:

Am7   B♭6/9   C   F/A   B♭6/9
All my days I will sing this song of gladness

Am7   B♭6/9   C   F/A B♭sus2
Give my praise to the Fountain of delights

   Gm7   C   B♭sus2   C
For in my helplessness, You heard my cry

    Gm7   Am7   D/F♯   G
And waves of mercy poured down on my life

VERSE 2:

Am7   B♭6/9   C   F/A   B♭6/9
I   will trust in the cross of my Redeemer

Am7   B♭6/9   C   F/A B♭sus2
I   will sing of the blood that never fails

   Gm7   C   B♭sus2   C
Of sins forgiven, of conscience cleansed

    Gm7   Am7   G/B Am7 G
Of death defeated and life without end

CHORUS:

            C/E   F   G   C
Beautiful Savior,   Wonderful Counselor

            Dm7
Clothed in majesty, Lord of history

            G/B   Am7   G
You're the Way, the Truth, the Life

            C/E   F   G   C
Star of the Morning,   glorious in holiness

            Dm7
You're the Risen One, heaven's champion

      G/B Am7 G   Am7   B♭6/9   C (2 bars)
And You reign, You reign (over all)

VERSE 3:

   Am7   B♭6/9   C   F/A B♭6/9
I long to be where the praise is never-ending

Am7   B♭6/9   C   F/A B♭sus2
Yearn to dwell where the glory never fades

      Gm7   C   B♭sus2   C
Where countless worshippers will share one song

      Gm7   Am7   G/B Am7 G
And cries of "Worthy!" will honor the Lamb

(REPEAT CHORUS 2X)

TAG:

Am7   B♭6/9   C (2 bars)
(Vocal ad lib.)

DAYS OF ELIJAH

ROBIN MARK

Key of **G Major, 4/4**

INTRO (2X):

G   C   G   D

VERSE 1:

```
G                    C       G       D       G
These are the days of Elijah, declaring the word of the Lord
    G                           C           G       D   G
And these are the days of Your servant Moses, righteousness being restored
    Bm                          Em      Am      C       Dsus   D
And though these are days of great trials, of famine and darkness and sword
    G               C           G       D       G
Still we are the voice in the desert crying, "Prepare ye the way of the Lord!"
```

CHORUS:

```
    D       G                   C
Behold, He comes, riding on the clouds
            G               D
Shining like the sun at the trumpet call
    G                       C
Lift your voice, it's the year of Jubilee
            G   D   G   (C   G   D)
And out of Zion's hill salvation comes
```

VERSE 2:

```
    G               C       G       D       G
And these are the days of Ezekiel, the dry bones becoming as flesh
    G                       C       G   D   G
And these are the days of Your servant David, rebuilding a temple of praise
    Bm                      Em      Am      C       Dsus   D
And these are the days of the harvest, the fields are as white in Your world
    G               C           G       D       G
And we are the laborers in Your vineyard, declaring the word of the Lord
```

(REPEAT CHORUS 3X)

TAG:

```
D       G                   C
Lift your voice, it's the year of Jubilee
            G   D   G (hold)
And out of Zion's hill salvation comes
```

HOW GREAT IS OUR GOD

CHRIS TOMLIN, JESSE REEVES and ED CASH

Key of **G Major, 4/4**

INTRO:

G (2 bars)

VERSE 1:

     G   **Em7**
The splendor of the King, clothed in majesty

            Cmaj7
Let all the earth rejoice, all the earth rejoice

    G   **Em7**
He wraps Himself in light, and darkness tries to hide

          Cmaj7
It trembles at His voice, trembles at His voice

CHORUS:

     G
How great is our God. Sing with me

   Em7
How great is our God. All will see

  Cmaj7   **D**   **G**
How great, how great is our God

VERSE 2:

G   **Em7**
Age to age He stands, and time is in His hands

         Cmaj7
Beginning and the End, Beginning and the End

   G   **Em7**
The God-head, Three in One, Father, Spirit, Son

        Cmaj7
The Lion and the Lamb, the Lion and the Lamb

(REPEAT CHORUS)

BRIDGE:

G   **Em7**
Name above all names, worthy of all praise

  Cmaj7   **D**   **G**
My heart will sing: How great is our God!

      G   **Em7**
He's the Name above all names, worthy of all praise

  Cmaj7   **D**   **G**
My heart will sing: How great is our God!

(REPEAT CHORUS 2X)

LET MY WORDS BE FEW
(I'LL STAND IN AWE OF YOU)

MATT REDMAN and BETH REDMAN

Key of **G Major**, 4/4

INTRO:

G   G+   Em7   Csus2

VERSE 1:

G   G+   Em7   Csus2
   You are God in heaven, and here am I on earth

G   G+   Em7   Csus2
   So I'll let my words be few

Am7 Em7 Csus2 D   G
Jesus, I am so   in love with You

CHORUS:

       G   Fsus2 Em7   Am7 D7sus
And I'll stand in awe of You

       G   Fsus2 Em7   Csus2
Yes, I'll stand in awe of You

     Am7 Em7   Csus2
And I'll let my words be few

Am7 Em7 Csus2 D   (G)
Jesus, I am so   in love with You

VERSE 2:

G   G+   Em7   Csus2
   The simplest of all love songs I want to bring to You

G   G+   Em7   Csus2
   So I'll let my words be few

Am7 Em7 Csus2 D   G
Jesus, I am so   in love with You

(REPEAT CHORUS 2X)

TAG:

Am7 Em7   Csus2

Am7 Em7   Csus2 D
Jesus, I am so   in love with You

OUTRO:

G G+ Em7 C D G (hold)

NO ONE LIKE YOU

JACK PARKER, MIKE DODSON, JASON SOLLEY, MIKE HOGAN, JEREMY BUSH and DAVID CROWDER

Key of **G Major**, 4/4

INTRO (2X):

G   D   Em7   Csus2

VERSE 1:

G   **Em7**   **Dsus**   **Csus2**
You are more   beautiful   than anyone   ever

G   **Em7**   **Dsus**   **Csus2**
And ev'ry day   You're the same,   You never change,   no, never

G   **Em7**   **Dsus**   **Csus2**
And how could I   ever deny   the love of my   Savior?

G   **Em7**   **Dsus**   **Csus2**
You are to me   ev'rything,   all I need   forever

D   **C**
How could You be so good?

CHORUS:

G   **D** **Em7** **Csus2**
There is   no one like You

G   **D** **Em7** **Csus2**
There has never ever been anyone like You

INTERLUDE (2X):

G   D   Em7   Csus2

VERSE 2:

G   **Em7**   **Dsus**   **Csus2**
Ev'rywhere,   You are there,   earth or air,   surrounding

G   **Em7**   **Dsus**   **Csus2**
I'm not alone,   the heavens sing along.   My God, You're so   astounding

G   **Em7**   **Dsus**   **Csus2**
How could You be   so good to me?   Eternally, I believe

(REPEAT CHORUS 2X)

(REPEAT INTERLUDE)

BRIDGE:

Dsus   **Csus2**   **Dsus**   **Csus2**
How could You be so good to me?

Dsus   **Csus2**   **Dsus**   **Csus2**
How could You be so good to me?

Dsus   **Csus2**
We're not alone,   so sing along

Dsus   **Csus2**
We're not alone,   so sing along, sing along, sing along

(REPEAT CHORUS 4X)

END ON G

WONDERFUL MAKER

MATT REDMAN and CHRIS TOMLIN

Key of **G Major, 4/4**

INTRO:

G/B C(add2)   Em7   G/B

VERSE 1:

C(add2)
You spread out the skies over empty space

Em7   C(add2)   D/F♯   G/B
Said, "Let there be light;" to a dark and formless world Your light was born

VERSE 2:

C(add2)
You spread out Your arms over empty hearts

Em7   C(add2)   D
Said, "Let there be light;" to a dark and hopeless world Your Son was born

PRE-CHORUS:

   Am7   G/B   C(add2)
You made the world and saw that it was good

   Am7   G/B   C(add2)   D/F♯
You sent Your only Son, for You are good

CHORUS:

          C(add2)   Em7
What a wonderful Maker, what a wonderful Savior

           C(add2)   D   G
How majestic Your whispers,   and how humble Your love

            C(add2)   Em7
With a strength like no other, and the heart of a Father

          C(add2)   D   G
How majestic Your whispers,   what a wonderful God

VERSE 3:

   C(add2)
No eye has fully seen how beautiful the cross

   Em7   C(add2)   D
And we have only heard the faintest whispers of how great You are

(REPEAT PRE-CHORUS)

(REPEAT CHORUS 2X)

TAG:

(G)   C(add2)   D   C(add2)   G (hold)
How majestic Your whispers,   what a wonderful God

YESTERDAY, TODAY AND FOREVER

VICKY BEECHING

Key of **D Major**, 4/4

INTRO:

D/F♯ G   Bm7 A

D/F♯ G   Bm7 A

VERSE 1:

G   Bm7
Everlasting God

      G   Bm7
The years go by, but You're unchanging

G   Bm7
In this fragile world

     G   Bm7
You are the only firm foundation

Em7   D/F♯
   Always loving, always true

G   Bm7   A
   Always merciful and good, so good

CHORUS:

D/F♯   G   Bm7   A
Yesterday, today and forever

D/F♯   G   Bm7   A
You are the same, You never change

D/F♯   G   Bm7   A
Yesterday, today and forever

Em7   G   A
You are faithful and we will trust in You

(REPEAT INTRO) – *Vocal ad lib.*

VERSE 2:

G   Bm7
Uncreated One

     G   Bm7
You have no end and no beginning

G   Bm7
Earthly powers fade

     G   Bm7
But there is no end to Your Kingdom

Em7   D/F♯
   Always loving, always true

G   Bm7   A
   Always merciful and good, so good

(REPEAT CHORUS 2X)

INTERLUDE:

G   D/F♯   G   D/F♯
(Vocal ad lib.)

BRIDGE:

G   D/F♯
Yahweh, God unchanging

G   D/F♯
Yahweh, firm foundation. You are

G   D/F♯
Yahweh, God unchanging

G   D/F♯
Yahweh, firm foundation

(REPEAT CHORUS 2X)

OUTRO (4X):

D/F♯   G   Bm7   A
(Vocal ad lib.)

END ON D